ESSENTIAL
CISM

Exam Quiz

Updated for the
15th Edition Review Manual

Phil Martin

Copyright © 2018. All rights reserved. Except as permitted under the Copyright Act of 1976, no part of this publication may be reproduced or distributed in any form or by any means, or stored in a database or retrieval system, without the prior written permission of the publisher.

ISBN 978-1-98074-701-7

Essential CISM Exam Quiz

How to Use This Book

What this book is NOT:

An exam simulation.

What this book IS:

A way to make sure you know the material, so you will pass the exam.

Over 800 terms, definitions and questions covering all four CISM domains are presented in this one book. Each 'prompt' will be in one of three formats:

- Given a term, provide the definition
- Given the definition, provide the term
- Given a question, provide the best answer

The book is laid out in a 2-page format – the left page will contain the prompt, and the right page will contain the answer. Each prompt has a unique number so that you can easily match the prompt on the left page to the answer on the right page. Simply cover the right page with a piece of paper and slide it down to reveal the answer as you work your way down the left page. That will prevent your prying eyes from 'accidentally' peeking at the answer!

The content is presented in two sections. Section 1 contains the material in the order that the Essential CISM Exam Guide book presents it, and Section 2 presents the same material but in a randomized order. This will prevent you from inferring the correct answer based on nearby prompts.

Want to test your knowledge while driving/working out/base jumping? Just download the audio version from Audible, Amazon or iTunes!

An audio version of this print book is available on audible.com

Section 1

This first section will cover all material in the order it is presented in the accompanying Essential CISM Exam Guide book. This should make it easier to locate the relevant sections in the guide if you need to review specific content. However, at times the correct answer to a prompt may have been given away by a previous prompt. That is why it is important to test yourself using Section 2 (which has been randomized) once you feel you have mastered this section.

1	Define: Principle of Least Privilege
2	Define: Need-to-Know
3	Define: Segregation of Duties
4	Define: Criticality
5	Define: Sensitivity
6	Define: Assurance
7	Define: Total Cost of Ownership
8	Define: Governance
9	Define: Goal
10	Define: Strategy
11	Define: Policy
12	What term represents the part of an organization's 'constitution'?
13	Define: Sub-Policy
14	What are 5 attributes a good policy will possess?
15	What term represents the 'laws' of an organization?
16	Define: Standard
17	Define: Exception Process
18	Define: Procedure
19	What four things must a procedure define?

1	An approach that segments all resources so that we can increase access as-needed
2	A security approach that requires a person to not only have the proper authority to access resources, but also a valid need to do so
3	A security mechanism that prevents a single role from having too much power
4	The impact that the loss of an asset will have, or how important the asset is to the business
5	The impact that unauthorized disclosure of an asset will have
6	Being able to manage security risks by keeping vulnerabilities and threats to a level that we can live with
7	Represents the true cost to own an asset, as opposed to just the cost to initially acquire it
8	The act of creating a plan on how a company will achieve a goal and then making sure everyone executes that plan
9	The result we want to achieve
10	A plan of action to achieve a goal
11	A high-level statement of what senior management expects and will dictate the direction in which we are heading
12	Policy
13	A method to address a need separate from the bulk of the organization
14	<ul><li>It describes a strategy</li><li>It is a single general mandate</li><li>It is clearly and easily understood</li><li>It is only a few sentences long</li><li>It belongs to a set that is no more than two dozen in number</li></ul>
15	Standards
16	Tells us how to carry out a policy
17	Created when we encounter a standard for which we cannot create a process
18	An unambiguous list of steps required to accomplish a task
19	<ul><li>Required conditions before execution</li><li>Information displayed</li><li>The expected outcome</li><li>What to do when the unexpected happens</li></ul>

20	If a procedural task is mandatory, what terms should we use?
21	If a procedural task is preferred, what term should we use?
22	If a procedural task is discretionary, what terms should we use?
23	What can tend to weaken a procedure?
24	Define: Guideline
25	What do you get when you combine overconfidence with optimism?
26	Define: Anchoring
27	Define: Status Quo Bias
28	Define: Endowment Effect
29	Define: Mental Accounting Effect
30	Define: Herding Instinct
31	Define: False Consensus
32	Define: Confirmation Bias
33	Define: Selective Recall
34	Define: Biased Assimilation
35	Define: Biased Evaluation
36	Define: Groupthink
37	Define: Resources
38	Define: Constraints
39	Define: Risk Appetite
40	Define: Risk Tolerance
41	Define: Risk Capacity

20	'Must' and 'shall'
21	'Should'
22	'May' and 'can'
23	Too many uses of discretionary tasks
24	Contains information that is helpful when executing procedures
25	Estimates that are unrealistically precise and overly optimistic
26	The tendency to tie future estimates to a past estimate, even if there is no link between the two numbers.
27	A phenomenon in which a person will favor a known approach even when it has been demonstrated to be vastly ineffective
28	The tendency for people to hold something they already own at a higher value than if they did not already own it
29	Seen when we treat money differently based on where it comes from or how it is spent, and is common in boardrooms
30	The tendency for people to 'do what everyone else is doing'
31	The tendency to overestimate the extent to which other people share our own views or beliefs
32	Occurs when we seek opinions and facts that support a conclusion we have already reached
33	Occurs when we remember only facts and experiences that support our current assumptions
34	Encountered when we accept only facts that support our current position or perspective
35	Similar to Biased Assimilation, but we go one step further and attack anyone presenting facts that conflict with our own
36	Encountered when we experience pressure for agreement in team-based cultures.
37	Mechanisms, processes and systems that are available for use
38	Factors that work against efficiency
39	The amount of risk a business is willing to incur
40	The amount of deviation from the risk appetite a business considers acceptable
41	The amount of risk a business can absorb without ceasing to exist

42	What is the relationship between risk appetite, tolerance and capacity?
43	Define: Risk Acceptance
44	Define: Guideline
45	If there is risk associated with taking some kind of action, is there also risk associated with not taking that action?
46	What might happen if we mitigate a risk?
47	Define: Business Interruption Insurance
48	Define: Residual Risk
49	Define: Risk Analysis
50	What five actions take place during risk analysis?
51	What three techniques does risk analysis include?
52	What are five methods we can use to analyze risk?
53	Define: Qualitative Analysis
54	Define: Semiquantitative Analysis
55	Define: Quantitative Analysis
56	For value at risk, or VAR, to be useful, what do we have to have a lot of?
57	Define: Operationally Critical Threat Asset and Vulnerability Evaluation, or OCTAVE

42	risk appetite + risk tolerance <= risk capacity
43	Occurs when an organization decides that no action is required for a specific risk
44	Put into effect to reduce risk
45	Yes.
46	Another risk will increase, or perhaps even be created
47	An insurance policy an organization purchases to cover itself in the event that RTO is exceeded.
48	The amount of risk left over after it has been mitigated
49	The act of identifying the level for a risk, understanding its nature, and determining potential consequences
50	<ul><li>Examine all risk sources</li><li>Determine exposure</li><li>Determine consequences</li><li>Determine likelihood</li><li>Identify all existing controls</li></ul>
51	<ul><li>Interviews</li><li>Simulations</li><li>Analysis</li></ul>
52	<ul><li>Qualitative Analysis</li><li>Semiquantitative Analysis</li><li>Quantitative Analysis</li><li>Value at Risk</li><li>Operationally Critical Threat Asset and Vulnerability Evaluation (OCTAVE)</li></ul>
53	A risk approach in which the magnitude of the impact and likelihood of the potential consequences are arranged on a 2-dimensional matrix
54	A risk approach where we use categories to represent levels of risk using a numerical value
55	A risk approach in which numbers are assigned to both impact and likelihood
56	Historical data that is very accurate
57	A risk approach that is great when we need a well-established process to identify, prioritize and manage risk

58	What are the three phases that OCTAVE contains?
59	Define: Bayesian Analysis
60	Define: Bow Tie Analysis
61	Define: Delphi Method
62	Define: Event Tree Analysis
63	Define: Fault Tree Analysis
64	Define: Markov Analysis
65	Define: Monte-Carlo Analysis
66	Define: Vulnerability
67	Define: Exploit
68	Define: Threat
69	Define: Threat agent
70	What are the three types of threats?
71	Define: Risk
72	Define: Exposure
73	Define: Defense-In-Depth
74	What are the three types of threats we most often encounter?

58	• Locate all assets and build a threat profile • Locate all network paths and IT components required for each asset • Assign risk to each asset and decide what to do about it
59	A risk approach that looks at historical data and calculates the probability of risk
60	A risk approach that creates a visual diagram with the cause of an event in the middle, representing the 'knot' of a bow tie, with triggers, controls and consequences branching off of the 'knot'.
61	A risk approach that arrives at a consensus by asking a question to a group, tallying and revealing the anonymous results to the entire group, and then repeating until there is agreement.
62	A risk approach that is a bottom-up model that attempts to predict the future by reasoning through various events and calculating the probability of possible outcomes
63	A risk approach that is a top-down model where we start with an event and look for possible causes for that event to occur
64	A risk approach that assumes future events are not necessarily tied to past events; in this way we can examine systems that can exist in multiple states simultaneously
65	A risk approach that combines known risk with sources of uncertainty and calculates possible outcomes
66	A weakness in a system that allows a threat to compromise security
67	Occurs when a vulnerability is taken advantage of by an attacker
68	The danger that a vulnerability might be exploited
69	A person or process that exploits a vulnerability
70	Natural, manmade or technical
71	The likelihood that a threat agent will exploit a vulnerability combined with the damage that could result
72	A single real-world instance of a vulnerability being exploited by a threat agent
73	The application of multiple control layers such that if a layer fails, it does not cause the failure of the next layer as well
74	• Environmental • Technical • Man-made

75	Define: Environmental Threat
76	Define: Technical Threat
77	Define: Man-Made Threat
78	What are one of the greatest sources of man-made threats?
79	What is the first step to mitigate internal threats?
80	Define: Zero-Day Vulnerability
81	Define: Advanced Persistent Threat (APT)
82	What are the six steps in a typical APT attack?
83	What are the five most common sources for APTs?
84	Define: Emerging Threat
85	Define: Predisposing Conditions
86	Define: Vulnerability Management
87	Define: Probability
88	Define: Volatility
89	Define: Velocity
90	Define: Proximity
91	Define: Interdependency

75	A type of threat such as natural disasters
76	A type of threat that includes fire, electrical failure, gas or water leakage
77	A type of threat that results from man-made actions
78	Employees
79	The hiring process itself by reviewing references and background checks
80	A weakness that is so new a fix is not yet available
81	A skilled external attacker who is willing to invest considerable time and resources into bypassing an organization's network and system security controls.
82	<ul><li>Initial compromise</li><li>Establish foothold</li><li>Escalate privileges</li><li>Internal reconnaissance</li><li>Move laterally</li><li>Maintain presence</li><li>Complete the mission</li></ul>
83	<ul><li>Intelligence agencies</li><li>Criminal groups</li><li>Terrorist groups</li><li>Activist groups</li><li>Armed forces</li></ul>
84	Mounting evidence that something nefarious is going on in the organization's network and systems
85	Scenarios which may lead to the rapid or unpredictable emergence of new vulnerabilities
86	Part of the incident management capability represented by proactive identification, monitoring and repair of any weakness
87	The likelihood that a threat will exploit a vulnerability
88	A measure of how stable the conditions giving rise to risk are.
89	Measures two intervals - the amount of time from warning to the actual event, and the time from the actual event and subsequent impact
90	Indicates the time between an event and impact
91	Measures the correlation of multiple risk events

92	Define: Motivation
93	Define: Skill
94	Define: Visibility
95	What are some of the best controls?
96	Define: Risk Register
97	What are the four options for addressing risk?
98	Can we transfer financial impact of a risk?
99	Can we transfer legal impact of a risk?
100	Define: Inherent Risk
101	Define: Impact
102	What are the three ways in which we can group controls?
103	What are the three control methods?
104	What are the five control categories?

92	Measures the type of motivation the attacker has
93	Measures the proficiency of the attacker and informs us of potential targets
94	An attribute attached to the target
95	- Strong access controls - Limiting access to need-to-know - Network segmentation - Effective termination procedures - Good monitoring
96	A central list of all information security risks including specific threats, vulnerabilities, exposures and assets
97	- Accept - Mitigate - Avoid - Transfer
98	Yes
99	No
100	A risk prior to mitigation.
101	Caused when a threat exploits a vulnerability and causes a loss
102	- Methods - Categories - Technological categories
103	- Physical - Technical - Procedural
104	- Preventative - Detective - Corrective - Compensating - Deterrent

105	What are the three control technological categories?
106	Define: Preventative Control
107	Define: Detective Control
108	Define: Corrective Control
109	Define: Compensating Control
110	Define: Deterrent Control
111	Define: Procedural Control
112	Define: Administrative Control
113	Define: Managerial Control
114	Define: Technical Control
115	Define: Logical Control
116	Define: Physical Control
117	Define: Countermeasure
118	Define: General Control
119	Which is more efficient in terms of coverage - a countermeasure or general control?
120	Which is more effective - a countermeasure or general control?
121	What are the three steps to follow when selecting controls?
122	Define: Identity
123	Define: Authenticate
124	Define: Authorize
125	Define: Mandatory access control, or MAC

105	- Native - Supplemental - Support
106	A control that stops attempts to violate a security policy, such as access control, encryption or authentication
107	A control that warns us of attempted or successful violations of a security policy
108	A control that remediates or reverses an impact after it has been felt
109	A control that makes up for a weakness in another control
110	A control capable of providing warnings that can deter a potential compromise
111	A control that oversees or reports on a process and includes the procedures and operations of that process
112	Another name for a procedural control
113	Another name for a procedural control
114	A control that always contains some type of technology whether it is hardware or software
115	Another name for a technical control
116	A control that can physically restrict access to a facility or hardware
117	A control deployed to counter a specific threat known to exist
118	Any control that is not a countermeasure.
119	A general control
120	A countermeasure
121	- Determine acceptable risk and risk tolerance - Determine control objectives based on acceptable risk levels - Determine requirements for controls based on the objectives
122	Something that uniquely identifies the user, such as a user name, email address or thumbprint
123	Proving identity by providing something a person is, has or knows
124	Deciding the level of access to resources a user should be allowed based on the authenticated identity
125	A security access control that looks at the classification of the requested resource and compares it to the security clearance of the user

126	Which security access control is used in high-security implementations such as a military system?
127	Define: Discretionary access control, or DAC
128	Which security access control allows anyone with access to a resource to pass that access on to other users at their 'discretion'?
129	What are the two states a control can default to when it detects a malfunction?
130	Define: Fail Unsecure
131	Define: Fail Secure
132	Define: Compartmentalize to Minimize Damage
133	Define: Transparency
134	Define: Trust
135	Define: Trust No One
136	What two factors dictate the overall strength of a control?
137	What three considerations must be considered when evaluating control strength?
138	Define: Formal Control
139	Define: Native Control
140	Define: Supplemental Control
141	Define: Support Control

126	MAC
127	A security access control using groups to make security administration easier
128	DAC
129	Fail unsecure and fail secure
130	The behavior of a control when a failure is encountered and behaves as if the control were never in-place to begin with
131	The behavior of a control when a failure is encountered and locks down all access
132	An approach that groups resources into separate 'compartments', with each requiring a unique authorization control
133	Achieved when all stakeholders can easily understand how a security mechanism is supposed to work
134	Relevant to security means that we trust an external party to tell us if a user's identity has been authenticated and is valid
135	A design strategy that does not trust any one person to follow the proper procedures when administrating a system
136	• Inherent strength • Likelihood the control will be effective
137	• If it is preventative or detective • If it is manual or automated • If it has formal or ad-hoc
138	A control having documentation reflecting its procedures and how well it has been maintained
139	A control technology category representing out-of-the-box capabilities
140	A control technology category representing technology that is added to an information system after the fact
141	A control technology category representing technologies that automate a security-related procedure, process management information or increase management capabilities

142	Define: Annual Loss Expectancy, or ALE
143	Define: Asset Value, or AV
144	Define: Exposure Factor, or EF
145	Define: Single Loss Expectancy, or SLE
146	Define: Annualized Rate of Occurrence, or ARO
147	Define: Recovery Time Objective, or RTO
148	Define: Recovery Point Objective, or RPO
149	Define: Service Delivery Objective, or SDO
150	Define: Maximum Tolerable Outage, or MTO
151	Define: Maximum Tolerable Downtime, or MTD
152	Define: Allowable Interruption Window, or AIW
153	Define: Business Continuity
154	Define: Disaster Recovery
155	Define: Disaster Recovery Plan, or DRP
156	Define: Business Continuity Plan, or BCP
157	Define: Business Impact Analysis, or BIA
158	What is one of the downsides to a BIA?
159	What are the three primary goals for a BIA?

142	The amount of money we can expect to lose each year for a given risk
143	A monetary value assigned to an asset
144	The percentage of an asset's value that is likely to be destroyed by a given risk
145	The loss we will encounter if we experienced a single instance of a specific risk
146	The number of times a threat on a single asset is expected to happen in a single year
147	The maximum amount of time allowed to return compromised facilities and systems back to an acceptable level of operation
148	The amount of data we can stand to permanently lose in case of interruption in terms of time, usually hours or days.
149	The minimum level of service that must be restored after an event until normal operations can be resumed
150	The maximum time that an organization can operate in an alternate or recovery mode until normal operations are resumed
151	Another name for MTO
152	The amount of time normal operations can be down before the organization faces major financial problems that threaten its existence
153	A strategy to prevent, recover and continue from disasters
154	The recovery of IT systems after a disruption
155	A plan that documents how we will quickly restore data, applications and core services that run our business after a serious event happens
156	A plan that documents how an organization will prevent disruptions and continue operating at a strategical level with minimal or no downtime after a serious event happens
157	An analysis that helps us to understand what assets are important, and what their loss will mean to us
158	All assessments tend to be 'worse-case' and end up being inflated
159	• Prioritize the criticality of business process • Estimate the amount of downtime • Identify resource requirements

160	Define: Business Recovery
161	What are the seven phases typically included in BCP planning?
162	What comprises the total cost of the recovery process?
163	In BCP, what are three strategies to proactively address threats?
164	Define: Recovery Site
165	Define: Hot Site
166	Define: Warm Site
167	Define: Cold Site
168	Define: Mobile Site
169	Define: Duplicate Site
170	Define: Mirror Site
171	Define: Reciprocal Agreement

160	The recovery of all critical business processes required to resume operations
161	- Conducting a risk assessment or a BIA
- Defining a response and recovery strategy
- Documenting response and recovery plans
- Training that covers response and recovery procedures
- Updating response and recovery plans
- Testing response and recovery plans
- Auditing response and recovery plans
162	- Preparing for possible disruptions before a crisis
- Putting equipment and facilities into effect during a crisis
- Business interruption insurance
163	- Eliminate or neutralize a threat
- Minimize the likelihood of a threat
- Minimize the effects of a threat
164	A location where we move operations after the original site has been compromised
165	A recovery site that is fully configured and can be ready to operate in a number of hours
166	A recovery site that has the complete infrastructure ready to go, but usually is not able to operate at the capacity of the original site
167	A recovery site that only provides the basic infrastructure with no servers or software, and can take up to multiple weeks to bring online
168	A recovery site that is a specially designed trailer that can be quickly moved to a business location when needed
169	A recovery site configured exactly like the primary site and can be anything from a hot site to a reciprocal agreement with another company
170	A recovery site that is an always active duplicate site
171	An agreement between one or more businesses that promise to share their data centers and systems in the event one of the partners experiences an outage

172	What are four factors to consider when deciding on the type of site to be used for recovery operations?
173	What three locations should have a copy of the recovery plan?
174	What are the six common methods for ensuring continuity of network services?
175	Define: Redundancy
176	Define: Alternative Routing
177	Define: Diverse Routing
178	Define: Long-Haul Network Diversity
179	Define: Last-Mile Circuit Protection
180	Define: Voice Recovery
181	Define: Direct Attached Storage, or DAS
182	Define: Network Attached Storage, or NAS
183	Define: Storage Area Network, or SAN
184	Define: Redundant Array of Inexpensive Disks, or RAID
185	What storage solutions can RAID be used with?
186	Define: Fault-Tolerant

172	<ul><li>AIW, RTO, RPO, SDO and MTO</li><li>The distance to potential hazards</li><li>The distance between the primary and alternate sites</li><li>The nature of probable disruptions</li></ul>
173	The recovery site, a media storage facility, and at the homes of key decision-makers
174	<ul><li>Redundancy</li><li>Alternative routing</li><li>Diverse routing</li><li>Long-haul network diversity</li><li>Last-mile circuit protection</li><li>Voice recovery</li></ul>
175	A network continuity method in which we provide fail-over systems
176	A network continuity method that routes information through an alternate medium such as copper cable or fiber optics
177	A network continuity method that routes traffic through split or duplicate cables
178	A network continuity method that subscribes to two or more network service providers at the same time
179	A network continuity method that protects the communications infrastructure connected directly to a facility
180	A network continuity method that provides redundancy for voice lines
181	A data storage device that is connected directly to a server or client
182	A storage device that is a self-contained server, usually running some flavor of Linux, and is accessed through a network connection
183	A self-contained network that provides mass storage using any number of internal media such as hard drives, optical disks or tape drives
184	A disk configuration providing great redundancy and performance improvements by writing data to multiple disks simultaneously
185	DAS, NAS or SAN solutions
186	A storage solution in which the primary system communicates in real-time with the fail-over system

187	Define: Load Balancing
188	Define: Clustering
189	When using load balancing or clustering, what must we be careful to do?
190	Define: High-Availability
191	Define: Cybersecurity Insurance
192	Define: Professional and Commercial Liability Insurance
193	Define: Extra Expense Policy
194	Define: Business Interruption Insurance
195	Define: Valuable Papers and Records Policies
196	Define: Errors and Omissions Insurance
197	Define: Fidelity Coverage Policies
198	Define: Media Transportation Insurance
199	What four events can cause an update to the incident response plan?
200	How often should plans be tested?
201	What three items must the security manager take care of prior to a test?
202	What are the five steps when testing a plan?

187	A fault-tolerant configuration in which both the primary and fail-over systems process load during normal use, and on failure of either system the remaining system takes on all load.
188	Another name for load balancing
189	Ensure that all load can be handled by either system by itself
190	A storage solution in which we have two systems, but only one is in active use and the second is not necessarily kept up to date in real-time
191	Insurance that covers losses incurred as a result of a cyberattack
192	Insurance which protects a business from losses experienced as a result of third-party claims.
193	Insurance which reimburses to the business for expenses incurred in maintaining operations at a facility that experiences damage.
194	Insurance that reimburses lost profit because of an IT malfunction or security incident causing the loss of computing resources
195	Insurance that covers the actual cash value of papers and records that have been disclosed, or physically damaged or lost
196	Insurance that legally protects a business in case it commits an act, error or omission that results in a loss
197	Insurance that covers loss from dishonest or fraudulent acts by employees
198	Insurance that covers loss or damage to media during transport
199	<ul><li>Organizational strategy changes</li><li>New software applications</li><li>Software or hardware environment changes</li><li>Physical and environmental changes</li></ul>
200	At least once each year
201	<ul><li>The risk of disruption is minimized</li><li>The business accepts the risk of testing</li><li>The organization can restore operation at any point during testing</li></ul>
202	<ul><li>Develop test objectives</li><li>Execute the test</li><li>Evaluate the test</li><li>Create recommendations to improve effectiveness</li><li>Ensure recommendations are implemented</li></ul>

203	What are the five types of basic tests?
204	Define: Checklist Review Test
205	Define: Structured Walkthrough Test
206	Define: Simulation Test
207	Define: Parallel Test
208	Define: Full Interruption Test
209	What are the three categories of plan tests?
210	Define: Paper Tests
211	Define: Preparedness Test
212	Define: Full Operational Test
213	What are the three phases of a plan test?
214	Define: Pretest Phase
215	Define: Test Phase
216	Define: Posttest Phase
217	What are the four types of metrics we need to collect during testing?

| 203 | - checklist review
- Structured walkthrough
- Simulation
- Parallel
- Full interruption |
|---|---|
| 204 | A plan test in which all steps are reviewed |
| 205 | A plan test in which team members implement the plan on paper |
| 206 | A plan test in which team members role-play a simulated disaster without activating the recovery site |
| 207 | A plan test in which the recovery site is brought up to a state of operational readiness, but operations at the primary site continue |
| 208 | A plan test in which that activates the recovery site and shuts down the primary site. |
| 209 | - Paper
- Preparedness
- Full Operational |
210	A plan test category which covers checklist reviews and structured walkthroughs
211	A plan test category which covers simulation and parallel tests
212	A plan test category which is the same as a full interruption test
213	- Pretest
- Test
- Posttest
214	The plan test phase which sets the stage for the actual test
215	The plan test phase where the emergency is simulated, and people, systems and processes are moved to the recovery site to the extent the test allows
216	The plan test phase which cleans up after the test by returning people and assets to their correct location, disconnecting test equipment, and deleting company data from all third-party systems
217	- Elapsed time for completion of each major component
- The amount of work performed at the backup site
- Percentages that reflect the number of vital records, supplies and equipment successfully delivered to the backup site
- The accuracy of data entry and processing cycles at the recovery site

218	Define: Role
219	Define: Responsibility
220	Define: RACI Chart
221	What does RACI stand for?
222	Define: Skill
223	Define: Due Diligence
224	Define: Due Care
225	Define: Confidentiality
226	Define: Integrity
227	Define: Availability
228	Define: Authentication
229	Define: Nonrepudiation
230	Define: Access Control
231	Define: Privacy
232	Define: Compliance
233	Define: Key Goal Indicator, or KGI
234	Define: Critical Success Factor, or CSF
235	Define: Key Performance Indicator, or KPI
236	Define: Key Risk Indicator, or KRI
237	Define: Adware
238	Define: Antispam Device
239	Define: Antivirus

218	A title given to someone based on their job function
219	A description of something that a person with that role is expected to accomplish
220	A 2-dimensional matrix that lists roles on one axis, and responsibilities on another axis
221	- Responsible - Accountable - Consulted - Informed
222	The training, expertise and experience an individual has for a given role
223	Shown when we purposefully try and discover things that can go wrong
224	Shown when we act to ensure things don't go wrong
225	Prevents unauthorized disclosure of information
226	The ability to protect information from improper modification
227	A measure of how accessible an IT system or process is to its end users
228	The action of proving who we claim we are
229	A situation in which we cannot deny having sent a message
230	The act of controlling who has access to sensitive information based on their identity
231	Freedom from unwanted intrusion or disclosure of information.
232	The act of measuring policies, procedures and controls to ensure they are being enacted and effective
233	A value that tells us after the fact if an IT process has achieved its goal
234	An element or event that must occur if we are to reach a KGI
235	A value that tells us how well a process is performing relative to reaching a goal
236	Some type of behavior, activity or event that usually is accompanied by a rise in risk levels
237	Unwanted software that is annoying but normally harmless
238	A server component designed to detect and delete email SPAM
239	Software that runs on a computer and detects malicious software either attempting to install or that have already been installed

240	Define: Command and Control (C&C)
241	Define: Firewall
242	Define: Gateway
243	Define: Intrusion Detection System, or IDS
244	Define: Intrusion Prevention System, or IPS
245	Define: One-Way Hash
246	Define: PKI
247	Define: Malware
248	Define: Router
249	Define: Spyware
250	Define: Virtualization
251	Define: VoIP
252	Define: The Committee of Sponsoring Organizations of the Treadway Commission, or COSO
253	Define: The International Organization for Standardization, or ISO
254	Define: ISACA
255	Define: The International Information Systems Security Certification Consortium, Inc., or (ISC)2
256	Define: The US National Institute of Standards and Technology, or NIST
257	Define: The Sarbanes-Oxley Act (SOX)
258	Define: The Health Insurance Portability and Accountability Act, or HIPAA

240	A term used to describe a central command point from which all other activities are directed
241	A network device that limits traffic to certain IP addresses and ports
242	A firewall that links two networks together
243	A network device that looks for patterns indicative of an attack and sends out alerts
244	An IDS that will actively try and stop an attack that is underway
245	Used primarily to encrypt passwords in a way that is unencryptable
246	Public key infrastructure; how SSL and TLS certificates work invisibly
247	Malicious software that a user installs without knowing its true evil purpose
248	Allows separate networks to talk to each other by 'routing' the traffic between them
249	A form of malware but specifically watches whatever the user does, usually to steal credentials
250	A way to create a computer in-memory, such that multiple virtual computers are running simultaneously on one physical computer
251	Voice over IP; the protocol that soft phones use
252	An organization providing a framework called the 'COSO Framework'.
253	An organization authoring the ISO 2000 series, of which ISO 27001 and ISO 27002 are ones the most frequently used
254	An organization who owns the CISM certification, and who has created the Risk IT Framework.
255	An organization that owns multiple other security certifications, such as the CISSP.
256	An organization providing quite a number of standards and frameworks, most notably NIST 800-30 and NIST 800-39
257	A US federal law passed in 2002 that puts requirements on all publicly traded businesses to encourage transparency
258	A US federal law passed in 1996 to protect the privacy of a patient's medical information

259	Define: The Federal Information Security Modernization Act, or FISMA
260	Define: The Control Objectives for Information and Related Technologies, or COBIT
261	What are the five key principles that COBIT is based on?
262	Define: COBIT 5 Enabler
263	Define: COBIT 5 Goals Cascade
264	What are the seven categories of COBIT 5 enablers?
265	Define: COBIT 5 Process Assessment Model (PAM)
266	What are the six COBIT 5 PAM levels?
267	Define: ISO 27000 Series
268	What is the standard to which many organizations choose to be assessed and certified against?
269	Define: ISO 27001

259	A federal law passed in 2002 that provides a framework to protect federal agencies from security breaches
260	A framework created by ISACA and is geared specifically to IT
261	- Meeting stakeholder needs - Covering the enterprise end-to-end - Applying a single, integrated framework - Enabling a holistic approach - Separating governance from management
262	Factors that individually or collectively influence whether something will work
263	An approach where higher-level goals define what the different enablers should achieve
264	- Principles, policies and frameworks - Processes - Organizational structures - Culture, ethics and behavior - Information - Services, infrastructure and applications - People, skills and competencies
265	A tool used to capture both the current and future desired state for information security
266	- Level 0 - Incomplete Process - Level 1 - Performed Process - Level 2 - Managed Process - Level 3 - Established Process - Level 4 - Predictable Process - Level 5 - Optimizing Process
267	A set of standards to help organizations create and implement a valid security plan
268	The ISO 27000 series
269	Part of the ISO 27000 series that lays out requirements for an information security management system, or ISMS

270	Define: ISO 27002
271	Define: The Open Group Architecture Framework, or TOGAF
272	What are the four architecture domains in TOGAF?
273	Define: Business Architecture Domain
274	Define: Applications Architecture Domain
275	Define: Data Architecture Domain
276	Define: Technical Architecture Domain
277	Define: Architecture Development Method, or ADM
278	What are the 10 components in TOGAF ADM?
279	Define: Capability Maturity Model Integration, or CMMI

270	Part of the ISO 27000 series that provides best practices for information security controls
271	A framework for enterprise architecture that covers four areas, called architecture domains
272	- Business architecture - Applications architecture - Data architecture - Technical architecture
273	The TOGAF architecture domain which defines the business strategy, governance, organization and key business processes
274	The TOGAF architecture domain which provides a blueprint for the systems to be deployed, and describes their interaction and how they relate to business processes
275	The TOGAF architecture domain which describes the structure of logical and physical data, and management resources
276	The TOGAF architecture domain which describes the hardware, software and networks needed to implement applications
277	A portion of TOGAF that is used to drive progress, and contains 9 phases and a central block
278	- Preliminary - Architecture vision - Business architecture - Information systems - Technology architecture - Opportunities and solutions - Migration planning - Implementation governance - Architecture change management - Central requirements management block
279	A framework that helps organizations reach an elevated level of performance

280	What are the five CMMI Levels?
281	Define: Balanced Scorecard
282	What are the four Balanced Scorecard perspectives?
283	Define: Information Technology Infrastructure Library, or ITIL
284	Define: Culture
285	What are the seven things that culture is comprised of?
286	What are the five steps in creating a culture?
287	Define: Metric
288	Define: Reference Point
289	Define: Measured Point

280	- Level 1 - Initial - Level 2 - Managed - Level 3 - Defied - Level 4 - Quantitatively Managed - Level 5 - Optimizing
281	A management system that helps organizations to create clear goals and translate them into action
282	- Learning and growth - Business process - Customer - Financial
283	A set of detailed practices for managing IT services with a special focus on aligning those services with the needs of business
284	The beliefs and resulting behaviors that are expected and are viewed as normal within the company
285	- Organizational behavior - How people influence the organization's structure so that work can get done - Attitudes - Norms - How well teams work together - The existence or lack of turf wars - Geographic dispersion
286	- Experience - Respond - Expected behavior - Unwritten rule - Normal
287	Created by comparing two data points to each other
288	Some type of a baseline represented by a known value taken at some point in the past
289	A measurement taken after a reference point later and is used to see how far off we are, or how far we have come

290	What does the SMART acronym stand for?
291	Beyond SMART, what other attributes comprise a good litmus test for metrics?
292	What are the three metric categories?
293	Define: Current State
294	Define: Desired State
295	Define: Gap Analysis
296	Define: Infrastructure
297	Define: Enterprise Information Security Architecture (EISA)
298	What are the three general categories of architectural approaches?
299	Define: Process Models
300	Define: Frameworks
301	Define: Reference Models
302	What are the 5 views that both the SABSA and Zachman frameworks use?
303	Define: Cloud Computing

| 290 | - Specific
- Measurable
- Attainable
- Relevant
- Timely |
|---|---|
| 291 | - Accurate
- Cost-Effective
- Repeatable
- Predictive
- Actionable |
| 292 | - Strategic
- Tactical
- Operational |
293	Where we are now
294	Where we want to be
295	An analysis of the work needed to get from the current state to the desired state
296	The foundation upon which information systems are deployed
297	An architecture designed to prevent ad-hoc, haphazard network architectures that are incredibly difficult to secure
298	- Process models
- Frameworks
- Reference models
299	An architectural category which dictates the processes used for each element
300	An architectural category which are very flexible and open
301	An architectural category which are actually small-scale representations of the actual implementation
302	- Contextual
- Conceptual
- Logical
- Physical
- Organizational
303	An approach to hosting applications somewhere in "the cloud" as opposed to being in a known location

304	What are the five essential characteristics of cloud computing?
305	Define: On-Demand Self-Service
306	Define: Elasticity
307	Define: Measured Service
308	Define: Infrastructure as a Service, or IaaS
309	Define: Platform as a Service, or PaaS
310	Define: Software as a Service, or SaaS
311	What are the four types of cloud deployment models?
312	Define: Private Cloud
313	Define: Community Cloud
314	Define: Public Cloud
315	Define: Hybrid Model
316	Define: Security as a Service, or SecaaS
317	Define: Disaster Recovery as a Service, or DRaaS
318	Define: Identity as a Service, or IDaaS
319	Define: Federated Identity
320	Define: Data Storage and Data Analytics as a Service

304	- On-demand self-service - Accessible over a broadband network - Computer resources are pooled - Elasticity - Measured service
305	Occurs when computing capabilities are provisioned without any type of human interaction
306	Occurs when resource can rapidly scale up or down in response to real-time business needs
307	Occurs when customers are charged-per-use
308	A cloud-based offering that provides the customer with a ready-made network, storage and servers
309	A cloud-based offering that manages operating systems, middleware and other run-time components
310	A cloud-based offering that is an application that someone hosts and maintains.
311	- Private cloud - Community cloud - Public cloud - Hybrid model
312	A network hosted entirely inside of a company's intranet and is not accessible externally.
313	A private cloud that a select few other companies can access
314	An application hosted across the Internet and publicly accessible
315	Occurs when a private cloud connects across the public Internet into another application
316	A cloud-based offering providing a way to outsource security processes
317	A cloud-based offering taking on the responsibility of hosting and maintaining a disaster recovery solution
318	A cloud-based offering for identity management
319	An identity solution when identity access management itself is hosted in the cloud
320	A cloud-based offering that delivers storage and analysis of huge amounts of data

321	Define: Cloud Access Security Brokers, or CASBs
322	Define: Information as a Service, or IaaS
323	Define: Integration Platform as a Service, or IPaaS
324	Define: Forensics as a Service, or FRaaS
325	What are two tools that help with selection of a cloud service provider?
326	Define: Strategic Metrics
327	Define: Management Metrics
328	Define: Tactical Metrics
329	Define: Operational Metrics
330	Define: Metametrics
331	Define: The Business Model for Information Security, or BMIS
332	Define: System Theory
333	Define: Systems Thinking
334	What are the four primary elements in BMIS?
335	Define: Organization
336	Define: Design
337	How do we get from strategy to design?

321	Tools that provide an easy and comprehensive way to secure the path between a company and hosted cloud services
322	A cloud-based offering that hosts and analyzes big data, requiring you to only ask a question
323	A cloud-based offering that comes into play when a hybrid cloud model is used
324	A cloud-based offering providing forensic tools and expertise
325	CSA Cloud Control Matrix and the Jericho Forum Self-Assessment Scheme
326	Metrics that provide the information necessary to guide decisions at the senior management level
327	Metrics that is used by the security manager to determine if the security program is remaining in compliance, is tackling emerging risk and is in alignment with business goals
328	Another name for management metrics
329	Metrics that are comprised of technical and procedural metrics such as existing vulnerabilities and the progress of our patch management processes
330	Attributes on metrics used to calculate an overall value for prioritization
331	A business-oriented approach to information security that models complex relationships using system theory
332	An approach that views a system as a complete functioning unit - not simply the sum of its parts
333	A thought method that drives us to study the results of interactions within a system
334	<ul><li>Organization</li><li>People</li><li>Process</li><li>Technology</li></ul>
335	A network of people, assets and processes interacting with each other in defined roles and working toward a common goal
336	How an organization implements strategy and includes processes, culture and architecture
337	By using resources

338	What four attributes must a process possess to be of value?
339	What is the BMIS dynamic relationship between Organization and Process?
340	What is the BMIS dynamic relationship between Organization and People?
341	What is the BMIS dynamic relationship between Process and Technology?
342	What is the BMIS dynamic relationship between Process and People?
343	What is the BMIS dynamic relationship People and Technology?
344	What is the BMIS dynamic relationship between Organization and Technology?
345	Define: Information
346	Define: Knowledge
347	Define: Data
348	What are the four different areas of governance?
349	Define: Enterprise Governance
350	Define: Corporate Governance
351	Define: Information Security Governance
352	Define: IT Governance
353	Define: GRC
354	Define: Risk Management
355	Define: Mitigation
356	Define: Compliance
357	Define: Criticality
358	Define: Sensitivity

338	<ul><li>Meet some type of business requirements</li><li>Be adaptable to changing requirements.</li><li>Be well documented</li><li>Be reviewed periodically</li></ul>
339	Governance
340	Culture
341	Enabling and Support
342	Emergence
343	Human Factors
344	Architecture
345	Data having meaning and purpose
346	Information that has been absorbed
347	Nothing but facts
348	<ul><li>Enterprise</li><li>Corporate</li><li>IT</li><li>Information Security</li></ul>
349	A process that watches over the entire organization or business
350	A process that sets the strategic direction of a business by defining goals
351	A process that is concerned with both business goals and how a business operates internally
352	A process that is concerned with all things IT
353	The trifecta of governance, risk management and compliance
354	The action of addressing known risks until they are at acceptable levels, identifying potential risks and associated impacts, and prioritizing both against our business goals
355	The act of reducing risk
356	The act of measuring policies, procedures and controls to ensure they are being enacted and effective
357	A measure of the impact if we lose control of information
358	A measure of the impact if we accidentally disclose information

359	Define: Steering Committee
360	Define: Governing Board and Senior Management
361	Define: Chief Risk Officer, or CRO
362	Define: Chief Information Officer, or CIO
363	Define: Chief Information Security Officer, or CISO
364	Define: Information Security Manager
365	Define: System and Information Owners
366	Define: Business and Functional Managers
367	Define: IT Security Practitioners
368	Define: Security Awareness Trainers
369	Define: Convergence
370	Define: Assurance Integration
371	What are the five factors driving convergence?
372	What are six elements of the initial business case?

359	A collective made up of senior representatives from all impacted groups
360	Those who must exercise due care and is ultimately responsible for ensuring sufficient resources are made available to address security risk
361	The person in charge of enterprise risk management
362	The person who handles IT planning, budgeting and performance
363	The person who performs the same functions as the security manager, but holds greater authority and reports to the CEO, COO or the board of directors
364	The person who is responsible for security programs creating a methodology to identify and manage risk, usually including IT systems
365	The people who ensure controls are in place to address CIA, and who must approve changes to IT systems
366	The managers responsible for business operations and the IT procurement processes
367	The people who interact with IT systems on a daily basis and enact changes as needed
368	The people who understand risk management goals and processes and create training materials and programs to spread this knowledge to the appropriate employees
369	The combination of physical and information security
370	Another name for convergence
371	<ul><li>Rapid expansion of the enterprise</li><li>The increasing value of information and intangible assets above physical assets</li><li>New technologies blurring functional boundaries</li><li>New compliance and regulatory requirements</li><li>The pressure to reduce cost</li></ul>
372	<ul><li>Project scope</li><li>Current analysis</li><li>Requirements</li><li>Approach</li><li>Evaluation</li><li>Review</li></ul>

374	Define: Kill Point
375	What are the four groups that need tailored communications?
376	Define: Architecture Framework
377	Define: Reference Architecture
378	Define: Enterprise Architecture Represents
379	Define: Enterprise Information Security Architecture, or EISA
380	What are the three things that all architecture frameworks seek to do?
381	Which architecture framework has enjoyed the most widespread acceptance globally?
382	What are 5 non-framework approaches used for developing and implementing a strategy?
383	What are the three types of measurements we can use for policies, standards and guidelines?
384	Why is a centralized information security approach the preferred method?
385	When does a decentralized information security approach works the best?
386	Define: Audit
387	What are the three types of insurance?

374	Another name for a stage gate
375	- Senior management - Business process owners - Other management personnel - Remaining employees
376	A foundation on top of which multiple architectures can be built
377	The architecture that is to be built
378	The foundation on top of which the entire company is built
379	A subset of enterprise architecture designed to give a jump-start on designing an information security program
380	- Detail the roles, entities and relationships that exist - Provide a taxonomy (naming conventions) for all processes that describes how they are executed and secured - Deliver a set of artifacts describing how a business operates and what security controls are required
381	COBIT 5
382	- ISO 9001 - Six Sigma - NIST publications - Information Security Forum (ISF) publications - US Federal Information Security Modernization Act (FISMA)
383	- Metrics - Boundaries - Processes
384	It provides the best alignment across all business units
385	When dealing with multinational companies with locations in different countries or legal jurisdictions
386	An activity used to determine information security deficiencies in terms of controls and compliancy
387	- First-Party - Third-Party - Fidelity

388	Define: First-Party Insurance
389	Define: Third-Party Insurance
390	Define: Fidelity Insurance
391	What are four types of third-parties entities?
392	What are four challenges when dealing with third-party entities?
393	What are two primary aspects to consider when deciding how long to keep business records?
394	Define: E-discovery
395	What are the six components of a governance framework?
396	What four things must a metric do to have true value?
397	What three metrics are the most useful as justification for expending resources?
398	Define: ISO 27004

388	Insurance that covers the organization from most sources and includes business interruption, direct loss and recovery costs
389	Insurance that covers liability with third-parties such as defense against lawsuits and damages
390	Insurance that protects against employee or agent theft and embezzlement
391	- Service providers - Outsourced operations - Trading partners - Merged or acquired organizations
392	- Cultural differences - Technology incompatibilities - How incidences are responded to - The level of acceptable BC and DR
393	- Business requirements - Legal and regulatory requirements
394	The location and delivery of information in response to a request in which the company is legally bound to comply with
395	- Strategy - Policies - Standards - Security organization - Workflows and structures - A way to measure compliance
396	- Deliver whatever is important to manage information security operations - Meet IT security management requirements - Meet the needs of business process owners - Provide what senior management wants to know
397	- VAR - ROSI - ALE
398	A standard that has not seen wide-spread acceptance and is currently being rewritten

399	Define: The Center for Internet Security, or CIS
400	Define: NIST SP 800-55
401	What are the four steps used to capture usable security metrics?
402	What is the best indicator of how well our security program is doing?
403	Define: Value Delivery
404	Define: Information Security Resource Management
405	What are the six outcomes that will tell us if our information security governance is working?
406	Define: Strategically Alignment
407	What three things must we accomplish to be strategically aligned?
408	Define: Risk Management
409	What are the three phases of risk assessment?
410	Define: Risk Identification Phase
411	Define: Risk Analysis Phase

399	An organization that released a document in 2010 called The CIS Security Metrics based on the consensus of 150 industry professionals
400	A standard that aligns with the security controls listed in NIST SP 800-53
401	• Strong Upper-Level Management Support • Practical Security Policies and Procedures • Quantifiable Performance Metrics • Results-Oriented Metrics Analysis
402	How much the negative impact of incidents experienced over a year exceed acceptable risk levels
403	Occurs when the investment in security provides the greatest support for business goals
404	The processes to plan, allocate and control resources
405	• Strategically aligned • Managing risk • Delivered value • Optimized resources • Measuring performance • Integration
406	Occurs when information security lines up with our business strategy
407	• The enterprise defines what good security looks like. • Security matches the company's DNA instead of trying to rewrite it. • The amount of money we spend on security accurately reflects how important security is to us.
408	The act of striking the right balance between taking advantage of opportunities for gain while minimizing the chances of loss
409	• Identification • Analysis • Evaluation
410	A phase of risk assessment where we create a list of vulnerabilities and take inventory of current threats
411	A phase of risk assessment where we take each risk and perform a BIA to come up with the possible impact

412	Define: Risk Evaluation Phase
413	What are the five phases of the system development life cycle, or SDLC?
414	What are the four steps of the risk management life cycle?
415	What are the five components of a good security review process?
416	What three things do audit 'work papers' accomplish?
417	Why does Enterprise Resource Planning, or ERP, systems deserve special attention?
418	What are 5 organizations dedicated to finding and reporting vulnerabilities?
419	Define: Compliance Enforcement
420	Define: Enforcement Procedure
421	Define: Policy Exception

412	A phase of risk assessment where we look at the impact from each risk and decide if it falls within an acceptable range based on our risk appetite, tolerance and capacity.
413	- Initiation
- Development and acquisition
- Implementation
- Operation or maintenance
- Disposal
414	- IT risk identification
- IT risk assessment
- Risk response and mitigation
- Risk and control monitoring and reporting
415	- An objective
- A scope
- A list of constraints
- An approach
- A result
416	- Maps controls to objectives
- Describes what the team did to test those controls
- Links the test results to the final assessment of effectiveness
417	Because the compromise of this single system can disrupt operations across the entire organization
418	- US Computer Emergency Readiness Team, or CERT
- MITRE's Common Vulnerabilities and Exposures database
- Security Focus's BUGTRAQ mailing list
- The SANS Institute
- OEMS
419	The act of making sure that an organization's security policies, standards and procedures are being followed
420	A procedure that makes sure another procedure is being followed
421	A means for business units or departments to request an exception to an existing policy

422	What four aspects should be considered for each threat evaluated?
423	What four things related to risk does a BIA do?
424	Define: Business Resource Dependency Assessment
425	What one thing does a Business Resource Dependency Assessment not provide that a BIA does provide?
426	What are the two types of outsourcing a security manager will have to deal with?
427	What are the two primary purposes for a contract?
428	Define: Right-To-Audit
429	Define: Right-To-Inspect
430	The frequency of third-party usage reviews is based on what three factors?
431	What three things does information systems architecture consider?
432	Define: Risk Management Strategy
433	What four things is the acceptable level of risk based on?

422	- If it is real - How likely it is to happen - How large the impact might be - Which systems, operations, personnel and facilities will be affected
423	- It determines the impact of losing the availability of any resource - It establishes the escalation of that loss over time - It identifies the resources needed to recover - It prioritizes the recovery of processes and supporting systems
424	A process that looks at all business functions, and for the most important figures out what resources are critical for that function to continue operating
425	The impact if resources are no longer available
426	- Third-parties providing security services - Outsourced IT or business processes that must be integrated into the information security program
427	- To clearly spell out rights and responsibilities - To provide a way to handle disagreements after the contract is signed
428	A contract clause allowing the customer to initiate an audit given sufficient notice to the vendor
429	A contract clause requiring little or no advanced notice of an inspection
430	- Criticality of information - Criticality of privileges - Length of the contract
431	- Goals - Environment - Technical skills
432	The plan to achieve risk management goals
433	- The ability to absorb loss - The risk appetite - The cost to achieve acceptable risk levels - Risk/benefit ratios

434	Define: Management
435	Define: Project Management Office, or PMO
436	What two attributes represent the business value of information assets?
437	What is the advantage of using a qualitative approach to assessing impact?
438	What is the disadvantage of using a qualitative approach to assessing impact?
439	What is the advantage of using a quantitative approach to assessing impact?
440	What is the disadvantage of using a quantitative approach to assessing impact?
441	Define: Aggregated Risk
442	Define: Cascading Risk
443	Define: Factor Analysis of Information Risk, or FAIR
444	What are the four elements of FAIR?
445	When dealing with risk taxonomy, what are four characteristics we need to look at?
446	Define: Probabilistic Risk Assessment, or PRA
447	What three questions does PRA ask?
448	Define: Risk Identification
449	Define: Exposure
450	What two factors does a viable threat possess?
451	Define: Systemic Risk

434	Achieving defined goals by bringing together human, physical and financial resources to make the best decisions
435	A department that oversees all projects
436	Sensitivity and criticality
437	It prioritizes risk and identifies areas for immediate improvement
438	It does not provide a measurable magnitude, making a cost-benefit analysis difficult
439	It supports a cost/benefit analysis
440	The quantitative meanings may be unclear, requiring a qualitative explanation
441	Occurs when a specific threat affects a large number of minor vulnerabilities
442	Occurs when a single failure leads to a chain reaction of other failures
443	An approach that allows us to decompose risk and understand the underlying components
444	<ul><li>Taxonomy</li><li>Method for measuring</li><li>Computational engine</li><li>Simulation model</li></ul>
445	<ul><li>The frequency with which threat agents contact assets at-risk</li><li>The probability of action by threat agents</li><li>The probability of success by threat agents</li><li>The type and severity of the impact to assets</li></ul>
446	A methodology to look at complex life cycles from concept to retirement
447	<ul><li>What can go wrong?</li><li>How likely is it?</li><li>What are the consequences?</li></ul>
448	The act of determining the type and nature of viable threats, and which vulnerabilities might be exploited by each threat
449	The potential loss when a vulnerability is exploited by a threat
450	<ul><li>They exist or could reasonably appear</li><li>They can be controlled</li></ul>
451	Represents a negative event affecting a large part of the area or industry

452	Define: Contagious Risk
453	What six attributes can be used to characterize a risk?
454	Why must care be taken with SOC 2 audits?
455	What five aspects should the level of security applied to hardware, software and information assets be based on?
456	What are the five components of a security management framework?
457	What are the processes involved with risk management?
458	Define: Baseline Security
459	What are the main two factors leading to improperly configured systems?
460	Define: Problem Management

452	Occurs when multiple failures happen within a very short time frame of each other
453	- Origin
- Threat
- Impact
- Specific reason for its occurrence
- Exposure and controls
- Time and place of occurrence
454	Because the outsourced provider is the one who defines the criteria
455	- Criticality of systems
- Sensitivity of information
- Significance of applications
- Cost of replacement hardware
- Availability of backup equipment
456	- Technical
- Operational
- Management
- Administrative
- Educational and Informational
457	- establish scope and boundaries,
- identify information assets and valuation
- perform the risk assessment,
- determine risk treatment or response
- accept residual risk,
- communicate about and monitor risk.
458	The minimum security level across the entire organization
459	- A lack of clear standards or procedures
- Shorthanded staff who take shortcuts
460	Finding the root cause of an emerging issue

461	What are the five steps involved in problem management?
462	What are the six areas program management must be evaluate?
463	What are the three most common ways to find out what capability we have for reporting incidents?
464	Define: Incident Response Plan, or IRP
465	What are the six phases to develop an incident response plan?
466	What are the minimum four things a BIA must do?
467	What three steps does the BIA follow?
468	Who is the most likely to be the first to receive an incident report?

461	- Understanding the issue - Defining the problem - Designing an action program - Assigning responsibility - Assigning due dates for resolution
462	- Program objectives - Compliance requirements - Program management - Security operations management - Technical security management - Resource levels
463	- Surveys - Using a self-assessment - Using an external assessment or audit
464	The operational component of incident management
465	- Preparation - Identification - Containment - Eradication - Recovery - Lessons learned
466	- Determine the loss resulting from some function no longer being available - Figure out how that loss will escalate over time - Identify the minimum resources needed to recover from that loss - Prioritize the recovery of processes and systems for all losses
467	- Gather assessment material - Analyze the information - Document the result and present recommendations
468	Help or service desk employees

469	What five teams are referenced by the incident response plan?
470	Define: Emergency Action Team
471	Define: Damage Assessment Team
472	Define: Relocation Team
473	Define: Security Team
474	Define: Emergency Management Team
475	What is the minimal training that incident response teams should go through?
476	Define: Red-Amber-Green Report
477	What four criteria should we look at when selecting individual KRIs?
478	What will be true when we have achieved effective risk management?
479	Define: Information Security Program

469	• Emergency action team • Damage assessment team • Relocation team • Security team • Emergency management team
470	An incident response team that deals with fires and other emergency scenarios
471	An incident response team that assesses the physical damage and decides what is a total loss or can be salvaged
472	An incident response team that moves operations from the affected site to an alternate site, and then back once the original site has been restored
473	An incident response team that takes care of all security concerns, including monitoring the security of systems and communications
474	An incident response team that coordinates the activities of all other teams and makes the key decisions
475	• Induction • Mentoring on roles, responsibilities and procedures • On-the-job training • Formal training
476	A report that uses color to quickly convey status
477	• The KRI should be an indicator for risks with high impacts. • If two or more KRIs are equivalent, choose the one that is easier to measure. • The KRI must be reliable in both predicting outcomes and having a high correlation with risk. • The KRI must be able to accurately model variances in the risk level with a high degree of sensitivity.
478	• We can handle complexity • Risk appetite and tolerance have been dictated by senior management • The information security manager has the authority to carry out his or her function • All Important assets have been identified, classified and have an owner • Assets have been prioritized
479	All activities and resources that provide information security services to an organization

480	When coming into a new environment, what is the best approach to get a handle on what needs to be done?
481	What is the most important aspect to consider with how the information security and IT departments report up through the organization?
482	What are the two most prevalent challenges facing a security manager?
483	To provide the best chance at success, what are the three areas in which a security manager should focus?
484	What are the five steps defined in CMU/SEI's Defining Incident Management Processes?
485	What three steps are required when measuring success?
486	What are the three categories that compliance requirements fall into?
487	Define: Statutory Compliance
488	Define: Contractual Compliance
489	Define: Internal Compliance
490	What are the four categories of resources?
491	Define: Assurance Provider
492	Define: Incident Handling

480	To first understand what those above expect, followed with an abundance of documentation on those expectations.
481	Each department must report up through a different executive to avoid conflict of interests.
482	- A view that security can be fixed with technology - Increased security simply makes my job harder
483	- Senior management support - Funding - Staffing
484	- Prepare - Protect - Detect - Triage - Respond
485	- Defining measurable goals - Tracking the most appropriate metrics - Periodically analyzing those results so we know where to make adjustments
486	- Statutory compliance - Contractual compliance - Internal compliance
487	Compliance in which external regulations and legislation demand compliance
488	Compliance where we are obligated by a contract to remain in compliance
489	Compliance in which we impose self-constraints for our own benefit
490	- Human - Financial - Technical - Knowledge
491	An individual or group that helps us to identify and manage risk in a specific area, as well as monitor the effectiveness of mitigation controls in that area.
492	A service that covers all processes or tasks associated with handling events and incidents

493	What four functions does incident handling involve?
494	Define: Incident Management
495	Define: Incident Response
496	What are two reasons that the security team possess some programming skills?
497	What is the last line of defense for cost-effective risk management?
498	What must incident management integrate with before it is of any value?
499	What is the goal of Incident management?
500	What are the five steps in incident management to effectively handle incidents?
501	What are two ways in which we can get senior management support?
502	What are the four incident response team models?
503	Define: Central IRT Model
504	Define: Distributed IRT Model
505	Define: Coordinating IRT Model

493	• Detection and reporting • Triage • Analysis • Incident response
494	Ensures that incidents are detected, recorded and managed to limit impacts
495	The last step in handling an incident, and carries out mitigation, containment, and recovery
496	• To be able to detect vulnerabilities • To be able to coach developers on secure coding practices
497	Incident management
498	Business processes and the BCP.
499	To prevent incidents from becoming problems, and problems from becoming disasters.
500	• Planning and preparation • Detection, triage and investigation • Containment, analysis, tracking and recovery • Post-incident assessment • Incident closure
501	• Wait for the unacceptable consequences of an incident to spur action • Create persuasive business cases detailing how similar incidents in peer organizations resulted in unacceptable consequences
502	• Central IRT model • Distributed IRT model • Coordinating IRT model • Outsourced IRT model
503	An incident response team model in which we have only one team
504	An incident response team model that supports multiple teams, each responsible for a different logical or physical segment of the infrastructure
505	An incident response team model in in which we have multiple distributed teams that manage and implement responses but rely upon a single central team providing all guidance and policy decisions

506	Define: Outsourced IRT Model
507	Define: Security Information and Event Manager, or SIEM
508	What are the two primary benefits of an SIEM?
509	Term: An approach that segments all resources so that we can increase access as-needed
510	Term: A security approach that requires a person to not only have the proper authority to access resources, but also a valid need to do so
511	Term: A security mechanism that prevents a single role from having too much power
512	Term: The impact that the loss of an asset will have, or how important the asset is to the business
513	Term: The impact that unauthorized disclosure of an asset will have
514	Term: Being able to manage security risks by keeping vulnerabilities and threats to a level that we can live with
515	Term: Represents the true cost to own an asset, as opposed to just the cost to initially acquire it
516	Term: The act of creating a plan on how a company will achieve a goal and then making sure everyone executes that plan
517	Term: The result we want to achieve
518	Term: A plan of action to achieve a goal
519	Term: A high-level statement of what senior management expects and will dictate the direction in which we are heading
520	Term: A method to address a need separate from the bulk of the organization
521	Term: Tells us how to carry out a policy
522	Term: Created when we encounter a standard for which we cannot create a process
523	Term: An unambiguous list of steps required to accomplish a task
524	Term: Contains information that is helpful when executing procedures

506	An incident response team model in we simply outsource at least a portion of the security team
507	A tool that gathers logs from across the network and combines the data into a single database
508	• Lower operating costs • Decreased response times to an event
509	Principle of Least Privilege
510	Need-to-Know
511	Segregation of Duties
512	Criticality
513	Sensitivity
514	Assurance
515	Total Cost of Ownership
516	Governance
517	Goal
518	Strategy
519	Policy
520	Sub-Policy
521	Standard
522	Exception Process
523	Procedure
524	Guideline

525	Term: The tendency to overestimate the extent to which other people share our own views or beliefs
526	Term: Occurs when we seek opinions and facts that support a conclusion we have already reached
527	Term: Occurs when we remember only facts and experiences that support our current assumptions
528	Term: Encountered when we accept only facts that support our current position or perspective
529	Term: Similar to Biased Assimilation, but we go one step further and attack anyone presenting facts that conflict with our own
530	Term: Encountered when we experience pressure for agreement in team-based cultures.
531	Term: Mechanisms, processes and systems that are available for use
532	Term: Factors that work against efficiency
533	Term: The amount of risk a business is willing to incur
534	Term: The amount of deviation from the risk appetite a business considers acceptable
535	Term: The amount of risk a business can absorb without ceasing to exist
536	Term: Occurs when an organization decides that no action is required for a specific risk
537	Term: Put into effect to reduce risk
538	Term: An insurance policy an organization purchases to cover itself in the event that RTO is exceeded.
539	Term: The amount of risk left over after it has been mitigated
540	Term: The act of identifying the level for a risk, understanding its nature, and determining potential consequences
541	Term: A risk approach in which the magnitude of the impact and likelihood of the potential consequences are arranged on a 2-dimensional matrix
542	Term: A risk approach where we use categories to represent levels of risk using a numerical value
543	Term: A risk approach in which numbers are assigned to both impact and likelihood

525	False Consensus
526	Confirmation Bias
527	Selective Recall
528	Biased Assimilation
529	Biased Evaluation
530	Groupthink
531	Resources
532	Constraints
533	Risk Appetite
534	Risk Tolerance
535	Risk Capacity
536	Risk Acceptance
537	Control
538	Business Interruption Insurance
539	Residual Risk
540	Risk Analysis
541	Qualitative Analysis
542	Semiquantitative Analysis
543	Quantitative Analysis

544	Term: A risk approach that is great when we need a well-established process to identify, prioritize and manage risk
545	Term: A risk approach that looks at historical data and calculates the probability of risk
546	Term: A risk approach that creates a visual diagram with the cause of an event in the middle, representing the 'knot' of a bow tie, with triggers, controls and consequences branching off of the 'knot'.
547	Term: A risk approach that arrives at a consensus by asking a question to a group, tallying and revealing the anonymous results to the entire group, and then repeating until there is agreement.
548	Term: A risk approach that is a bottom-up model that attempts to predict the future by reasoning through various events and calculating the probability of possible outcomes
549	Term: A risk approach that is a top-down model where we start with an event and look for possible causes for that event to occur
550	Term: A risk approach that assumes future events are not necessarily tied to past events; in this way we can examine systems that can exist in multiple states simultaneously
551	Term: A risk approach that combines known risk with sources of uncertainty and calculates possible outcomes
552	Term: A weakness in a system that allows a threat to compromise security
553	Term: Occurs when a vulnerability is taken advantage of by an attacker
554	Term: The danger that a vulnerability might be exploited
555	Term: A person or process that exploits a vulnerability
556	Term: The likelihood that a threat agent will exploit a vulnerability combined with the damage that could result
557	Term: A single real-world instance of a vulnerability being exploited by a threat agent
558	Term: The application of multiple control layers such that if a layer fails, it does not cause the failure of the next layer as well
559	Term: A type of threat such as natural disasters
560	Term: A type of threat that includes fire, electrical failure, gas or water leakage

544	Operationally Critical Threat Asset and Vulnerability Evaluation, or OCTAVE
545	Bayesian Analysis
546	Bow Tie Analysis
547	Delphi Method
548	Event Tree Analysis
549	Fault Tree Analysis
550	Markov Analysis
551	Monte-Carlo Analysis
552	Vulnerability
553	Exploit
554	Threat
555	Threat agent
556	Risk
557	Exposure
558	Defense-In-Depth
559	Environmental Threat
560	Technical Threat

561	Term: A type of threat that results from man-made actions
562	Term: A weakness that is so new a fix is not yet available
563	Term: A skilled external attacker who is willing to invest considerable time and resources into bypassing an organization's network and system security controls.
564	Term: Mounting evidence that something nefarious is going on in the organization's network and systems
565	Term: Scenarios which may lead to the rapid or unpredictable emergence of new vulnerabilities
566	Term: Part of the incident management capability represented by proactive identification, monitoring and repair of any weakness
567	Term: The likelihood that a threat will exploit a vulnerability
568	Term: A measure of how stable the conditions giving rise to risk are.
569	Term: Measures two intervals - the amount of time from warning to the actual event, and the time from the actual event and subsequent impact
570	Term: Indicates the time between an event and impact
571	Term: Measures the correlation of multiple risk events
572	Term: Measures the type of motivation the attacker has
573	Term: Measures the proficiency of the attacker and informs us of potential targets
574	Term: An attribute attached to the target
575	Term: A central list of all information security risks including specific threats, vulnerabilities, exposures and assets
576	Term: A risk prior to mitigation.
577	Term: Caused when a threat exploits a vulnerability and causes a loss
578	Term: A control that stops attempts to violate a security policy, such as access control, encryption or authentication
579	Term: A control that warns us of attempted or successful violations of a security policy
580	Term: A control that remediates or reverses an impact after it has been felt
581	Term: A control that makes up for a weakness in another control
582	Term: A control capable of providing warnings that can deter a potential compromise

561	Man-Made Threat
562	Zero-Day Vulnerability
563	Advanced Persistent Threat (APT)
564	Emerging Threat
565	Predisposing Conditions
566	Vulnerability Management
567	Probability
568	Volatility
569	Velocity
570	Proximity
571	Interdependency
572	Motivation
573	Skill
574	Visibility
575	Risk Register
576	Inherent Risk
577	Impact
578	Preventative Control
579	Detective Control
580	Corrective Control
581	Compensating Control
582	Deterrent Control

583	Term: A control that oversees or reports on a process and includes the procedures and operations of that process
584	Term: Another name for a procedural control
585	Term: Another name for a procedural control
586	Term: A control that always contains some type of technology whether it is hardware or software
587	Term: Another name for a technical control
588	Term: A control that can physically restrict access to a facility or hardware
589	Term: A control deployed to counter a specific threat known to exist
590	Term: Any control that is not a countermeasure.
591	Term: Something that uniquely identifies the user, such as a user name, email address or thumbprint
592	Term: Proving identity by providing something a person is, has or knows
593	Term: Deciding the level of access to resources a user should be allowed based on the authenticated identity
594	Term: A security access control that looks at the classification of the requested resource and compares it to the security clearance of the user
595	Term: A security access control using groups to make security administration easier
596	Term: The behavior of a control when a failure is encountered and behaves as if the control were never in-place to begin with
597	Term: The behavior of a control when a failure is encountered and locks down all access
598	Term: An approach that groups resources into separate 'compartments', with each requiring a unique authorization control
599	Term: Achieved when all stakeholders can easily understand how a security mechanism is supposed to work
600	Term: Relevant to security means that we trust an external party to tell us if a user's identity has been authenticated and is valid
601	Term: A design strategy that does not trust any one person to follow the proper procedures when administrating a system

583	Procedural Control
584	Administrative Control
585	Managerial Control
586	Technical Control
587	Logical Control
588	Physical Control
589	Countermeasure
590	General Control
591	Identity
592	Authenticate
593	Authorize
594	Mandatory access control, or MAC
595	Discretionary access control, or DAC
596	Fail Unsecure
597	Fail Secure
598	Compartmentalize to Minimize Damage
599	Transparency
600	Trust
601	Trust No One

602	Term: A control having documentation reflecting its procedures and how well it has been maintained
603	Term: A control technology category representing out-of-the-box capabilities
604	Term: A control technology category representing technology that is added to an information system after the fact
605	Term: A control technology category representing technologies that automate a security-related procedure, process management information or increase management capabilities
606	Term: The amount of money we can expect to lose each year for a given risk
607	Term: A monetary value assigned to an asset
608	Term: The percentage of an asset's value that is likely to be destroyed by a given risk
609	Term: The loss we will encounter if we experienced a single instance of a specific risk
610	Term: The number of times a threat on a single asset is expected to happen in a single year
611	Term: The maximum amount of time allowed to return compromised facilities and systems back to an acceptable level of operation
612	Term: The amount of data we can stand to permanently lose in case of interruption in terms of time, usually hours or days.
613	Term: The minimum level of service that must be restored after an event until normal operations can be resumed
614	Term: The maximum time that an organization can operate in an alternate or recovery mode until normal operations are resumed
615	Term: Another name for MTO
616	Term: The amount of time normal operations can be down before the organization faces major financial problems that threaten its existence
617	Term: A strategy to prevent, recover and continue from disasters
618	Term: The recovery of IT systems after a disruption
619	Term: A plan that documents how we will quickly restore data, applications and core services that run our business after a serious event happens

602	Formal Control	
603	Native Control	
604	Supplemental Control	
605	Support Control	
606	Annual Loss Expectancy, or ALE	
607	Asset Value, or AV	
608	Exposure Factor, or EF	
609	Single Loss Expectancy, or SLE	
610	Annualized Rate of Occurrence, or ARO	
611	Recovery Time Objective, or RTO	
612	Recovery Point Objective, or RPO	
613	Service Delivery Objective, or SDO	
614	Maximum Tolerable Outage, or MTO	
615	Maximum Tolerable Downtime, or MTD	
616	Allowable Interruption Window, or AIW	
617	Business Continuity	
618	Disaster Recovery	
619	Disaster Recovery Plan, or DRP	

620	Term: A plan that documents how an organization will prevent disruptions and continue operating at a strategical level with minimal or no downtime after a serious event happens
621	Term: An analysis that helps us to understand what assets are important, and what their loss will mean to us
622	Term: The recovery of all critical business processes required to resume operations
623	Term: A location where we move operations after the original site has been compromised
624	Term: A recovery site that is fully configured and can be ready to operate in a number of hours
625	Term: A recovery site that has the complete infrastructure ready to go, but usually is not able to operate at the capacity of the original site
626	Term: A recovery site that only provides the basic infrastructure with no servers or software, and can take up to multiple weeks to bring online
627	Term: A recovery site that is a specially designed trailer that can be quickly moved to a business location when needed
628	Term: A recovery site configured exactly like the primary site and can be anything from a hot site to a reciprocal agreement with another company
629	Term: A recovery site that is an always active duplicate site
630	Term: An agreement between one or more businesses that promise to share their data centers and systems in the event one of the partners experiences an outage
631	Term: A network continuity method in which we provide fail-over systems
632	Term: A network continuity method that routes information through an alternate medium such as copper cable or fiber optics
633	Term: A network continuity method that routes traffic through split or duplicate cables
634	Term: A network continuity method that subscribes to two or more network service providers at the same time
635	Term: A network continuity method that protects the communications infrastructure connected directly to a facility
636	Term: A network continuity method that provides redundancy for voice lines

620	Business Continuity Plan, or BCP
621	Business Impact Analysis, or BIA
622	Business Recovery
623	Recovery Site
624	Hot Site
625	Warm Site
626	Cold Site
627	Mobile Site
628	Duplicate Site
629	Mirror Site
630	Reciprocal Agreement
631	Redundancy
632	Alternative Routing
633	Diverse Routing
634	Long-Haul Network Diversity
635	Last-Mile Circuit Protection
636	Voice Recovery

637	Term: A data storage device that is connected directly to a server or client
638	Term: A storage device that is a self-contained server, usually running some flavor of Linux, and is accessed through a network connection
639	Term: A self-contained network that provides mass storage using any number of internal media such as hard drives, optical disks or tape drives
640	Term: A disk configuration providing great redundancy and performance improvements by writing data to multiple disks simultaneously
641	Term: A storage solution in which the primary system communicates in real-time with the fail-over system
642	Term: A fault-tolerant configuration in which both the primary and fail-over systems process load during normal use, and on failure of either system the remaining system takes on all load.
643	Term: Another name for load balancing
644	Term: A storage solution in which we have two systems, but only one is in active use and the second is not necessarily kept up to date in real-time
645	Term: Insurance that covers losses incurred as a result of a cyberattack
646	Term: Insurance which protects a business from losses experienced as a result of third-party claims.
647	Term: Insurance which reimburses to the business for expenses incurred in maintaining operations at a facility that experiences damage.
648	Term: Insurance that reimburses lost profit because of an IT malfunction or security incident causing the loss of computing resources
649	Term: Insurance that covers the actual cash value of papers and records that have been disclosed, or physically damaged or lost
650	Term: Insurance that legally protects a business in case it commits an act, error or omission that results in a loss
651	Term: Insurance that covers loss from dishonest or fraudulent acts by employees
652	Term: Insurance that covers loss or damage to media during transport
653	Term: A plan test in which all steps are reviewed
654	Term: A plan test in which team members implement the plan on paper

637	Direct Attached Storage, or DAS	
638	Network Attached Storage, or NAS	
639	Storage Area Network, or SAN	
640	Redundant Array of Inexpensive Disks, or RAID	
641	Fault-Tolerant	
642	Load Balancing	
643	Clustering	
644	High-Availability	
645	Cybersecurity Insurance	
646	Professional and Commercial Liability Insurance	
647	Extra Expense Policy	
648	Business Interruption Insurance	
649	Valuable Papers and Records Policies	
650	Errors and Omissions Insurance	
651	Fidelity Coverage Policies	
652	Media Transportation Insurance	
653	Checklist Review Test	
654	Structured Walkthrough Test	

655	Term: A plan test in which team members role-play a simulated disaster without activating the recovery site
656	Term: A plan test in which the recovery site is brought up to a state of operational readiness, but operations at the primary site continue
657	Term: A plan test in which that activates the recovery site and shuts down the primary site.
658	Term: A plan test category which covers checklist reviews and structured walkthroughs
659	Term: A plan test category which covers simulation and parallel tests
660	Term: A plan test category which is the same as a full interruption test
661	Term: The plan test phase which sets the stage for the actual test
662	Term: The plan test phase where the emergency is simulated, and people, systems and processes are moved to the recovery site to the extent the test allows
663	Term: The plan test phase which cleans up after the test by returning people and assets to their correct location, disconnecting test equipment, and deleting company data from all third-party systems
664	Term: A title given to someone based on their job function
665	Term: A description of something that a person with that role is expected to accomplish
666	Term: A 2-dimensional matrix that lists roles on one axis, and responsibilities on another axis
667	Term: The training, expertise and experience an individual has for a given role
668	Term: Shown when we purposefully try and discover things that can go wrong
669	Term: Shown when we act to ensure things don't go wrong
670	Term: Prevents unauthorized disclosure of information
671	Term: The ability to protect information from improper modification
672	Term: A measure of how accessible an IT system or process is to its end users
673	Term: The action of proving who we claim we are
674	Term: A situation in which we cannot deny having sent a message

655	Simulation Test
656	Parallel Test
657	Full Interruption Test
658	Paper Tests
659	Preparedness Test
660	Full Operational Test
661	Pretest Phase
662	Test Phase
663	Posttest Phase
664	Role
665	Responsibility
666	RACI Chart
667	Skill
668	Due Diligence
669	Due Care
670	Confidentiality
671	Integrity
672	Availability
673	Authentication
674	Nonrepudiation

675	Term: The act of controlling who has access to sensitive information based on their identity
676	Term: Freedom from unwanted intrusion or disclosure of information.
677	Term: The act of measuring policies, procedures and controls to ensure they are being enacted and effective
678	Term: A value that tells us after the fact if an IT process has achieved its goal
679	Term: An element or event that must occur if we are to reach a KGI
680	Term: A value that tells us how well a process is performing relative to reaching a goal
681	Term: Some type of behavior, activity or event that usually is accompanied by a rise in risk levels
682	Term: Unwanted software that is annoying but normally harmless
683	Term: A server component designed to detect and delete email SPAM
684	Term: Software that runs on a computer and detects malicious software either attempting to install or that have already been installed
685	Term: A term used to describe a central command point from which all other activities are directed
686	Term: A network device that limits traffic to certain IP addresses and ports
687	Term: A firewall that links two networks together
688	Term: A network device that looks for patterns indicative of an attack and sends out alerts
689	Term: An IDS that will actively try and stop an attack that is underway
690	Term: Used primarily to encrypt passwords in a way that is unencryptable
691	Term: Public key infrastructure; how SSL and TLS certificates work invisibly
692	Term: Malicious software that a user installs without knowing its true evil purpose
693	Term: Allows separate networks to talk to each other by 'routing' the traffic between them
694	Term: A form of malware but specifically watches whatever the user does, usually to steal credentials
695	Term: A way to create a computer in-memory, such that multiple virtual computers are running simultaneously on one physical computer

675	Access Control
676	Privacy
677	Compliance
678	Key Goal Indicator, or KGI
679	Critical Success Factor, or CSF
680	Key Performance Indicator, or KPI
681	Key Risk Indicator, or KRI
682	Adware
683	Antispam Device
684	Antivirus
685	Command and Control (C&C)
686	Firewall
687	Gateway
688	Intrusion Detection System, or IDS
689	Intrusion Prevention System, or IPS
690	One-Way Hash
691	PKI
692	Malware
693	Router
694	Spyware
695	Virtualization

696	Term: Voice over IP; the protocol that soft phones use
697	Term: An organization providing a framework called the 'COSO Framework'.
698	Term: An organization authoring the ISO 2000 series, of which ISO 27001 and ISO 27002 are ones the most frequently used
699	Term: An organization who owns the CISM certification, and who has created the Risk IT Framework.
700	Term: An organization that owns multiple other security certifications, such as the CISSP.
701	Term: An organization providing quite a number of standards and frameworks, most notably NIST 800-30 and NIST 800-39
702	Term: A US federal law passed in 2002 that puts requirements on all publicly traded businesses to encourage transparency
703	Term: A US federal law passed in 1996 to protect the privacy of a patient's medical information
704	Term: A federal law passed in 2002 that provides a framework to protect federal agencies from security breaches
705	Term: A framework created by ISACA and is geared specifically to IT
706	Term: Factors that individually or collectively influence whether something will work
707	Term: An approach where higher-level goals define what the different enablers should achieve
708	Term: A tool used to capture both the current and future desired state for information security
709	Term: A set of standards to help organizations create and implement a valid security plan
710	Term: Part of the ISO 27000 series that lays out requirements for an information security management system, or ISMS
711	Term: Part of the ISO 27000 series that provides best practices for information security controls
712	Term: A framework for enterprise architecture that covers four areas, called architecture domains

696	VoIP
697	The Committee of Sponsoring Organizations of the Treadway Commission, or COSO
698	The International Organization for Standardization, or ISO
699	ISACA
700	The International Information Systems Security Certification Consortium, Inc., or (ISC)2
701	The US National Institute of Standards and Technology, or NIST
702	The Sarbanes-Oxley Act (SOX)
703	The Health Insurance Portability and Accountability Act, or HIPAA
704	The Federal Information Security Modernization Act, or FISMA
705	The Control Objectives for Information and Related Technologies, or COBIT
706	COBIT 5 Enabler
707	COBIT 5 Goals Cascade
708	COBIT 5 Process Assessment Model (PAM)
709	ISO 27000 Series
710	ISO 27001
711	ISO 27002
712	The Open Group Architecture Framework, or TOGAF

713	Term: The TOGAF architecture domain which defines the business strategy, governance, organization and key business processes
714	Term: The TOGAF architecture domain which provides a blueprint for the systems to be deployed, and describes their interaction and how they relate to business processes
715	Term: The TOGAF architecture domain which describes the structure of logical and physical data, and management resources
716	Term: The TOGAF architecture domain which describes the hardware, software and networks needed to implement applications
717	Term: A portion of TOGAF that is used to drive progress, and contains 9 phases and a central block
718	Term: A framework that helps organizations reach an elevated level of performance
719	Term: A management system that helps organizations to create clear goals and translate them into action
720	Term: A set of detailed practices for managing IT services with a special focus on aligning those services with the needs of business
721	Term: The beliefs and resulting behaviors that are expected and are viewed as normal within the company
722	Term: Created by comparing two data points to each other
723	Term: Some type of a baseline represented by a known value taken at some point in the past
724	Term: A measurement taken after a reference point later and is used to see how far off we are, or how far we have come
725	Term: Where we are now
726	Term: Where we want to be
727	Term: An analysis of the work needed to get from the current state to the desired state
728	Term: The foundation upon which information systems are deployed
729	Term: An architecture designed to prevent ad-hoc, haphazard network architectures that are incredibly difficult to secure

713	Business Architecture Domain
714	Applications Architecture Domain
715	Data Architecture Domain
716	Technical Architecture Domain
717	Architecture Development Method, or ADM
718	Capability Maturity Model Integration, or CMMI
719	Balanced Scorecard
720	Information Technology Infrastructure Library, or ITIL
721	Culture
722	Metric
723	Reference Point
724	Measured Point
725	Current State
726	Desired State
727	Gap Analysis
728	Infrastructure
729	Enterprise Information Security Architecture (EISA)

730	Term: An architectural category which dictates the processes used for each element
731	Term: An architectural category which are very flexible and open
732	Term: An architectural category which are actually small-scale representations of the actual implementation
733	Term: An approach to hosting applications somewhere in 'the cloud' as opposed to being in a known location
734	Term: Occurs when computing capabilities are provisioned without any type of human interaction
735	Term: Occurs when resource can rapidly scale up or down in response to real-time business needs
736	Term: Occurs when customers are charged-per-use
737	Term: A cloud-based offering that provides the customer with a ready-made network, storage and servers
738	Term: A cloud-based offering that manages operating systems, middleware and other run-time components
739	Term: A cloud-based offering that is an application that someone hosts and maintains.
740	Term: A network hosted entirely inside of a company's intranet and is not accessible externally.
741	Term: A private cloud that a select few other companies can access
742	Term: An application hosted across the Internet and publicly accessible
743	Term: Occurs when a private cloud connects across the public Internet into another application
744	Term: A cloud-based offering providing a way to outsource security processes
745	Term: A cloud-based offering taking on the responsibility of hosting and maintaining a disaster recovery solution
746	Term: A cloud-based offering for identity management
747	Term: An identity solution when identity access management itself is hosted in the cloud
748	Term: A cloud-based offering that delivers storage and analysis of huge amounts of data

730	Process Models
731	Frameworks
732	Reference Models
733	Cloud Computing
734	On-Demand Self-Service
735	Elasticity
736	Measured Service
737	Infrastructure as a Service, or IaaS
738	Platform as a Service, or PaaS
739	Software as a Service, or SaaS
740	Private Cloud
741	Community Cloud
742	Public Cloud
743	Hybrid Model
744	Security as a Service, or SecaaS
745	Disaster Recovery as a Service, or DRaaS
746	Identity as a Service, or IDaaS
747	Federated Identity
748	Data Storage and Data Analytics as a Service

749	Term: Tools that provide an easy and comprehensive way to secure the path between a company and hosted cloud services
750	Term: A cloud-based offering that hosts and analyzes big data, requiring you to only ask a question
751	Term: A cloud-based offering that comes into play when a hybrid cloud model is used
752	Term: A cloud-based offering providing forensic tools and expertise
753	Term: Metrics that provide the information necessary to guide decisions at the senior management level
754	Term: Metrics that is used by the security manager to determine if the security program is remaining in compliance, is tackling emerging risk and is in alignment with business goals
755	Term: Another name for management metrics
756	Term: Metrics that are comprised of technical and procedural metrics such as existing vulnerabilities and the progress of our patch management processes
757	Term: Attributes on metrics used to calculate an overall value for prioritization
758	Term: A business-oriented approach to information security that models complex relationships using system theory
759	Term: An approach that views a system as a complete functioning unit - not simply the sum of its parts
760	Term: A thought method that drives us to study the results of interactions within a system
761	Term: A network of people, assets and processes interacting with each other in defined roles and working toward a common goal
762	Term: How an organization implements strategy and includes processes, culture and architecture
763	Term: Data having meaning and purpose
764	Term: Information that has been absorbed
765	Term: Nothing but facts
766	Term: A process that watches over the entire organization or business

749	Cloud Access Security Brokers, or CASBs
750	Information as a Service, or IaaS
751	Integration Platform as a Service, or IPaaS
752	Forensics as a Service, or FRaaS
753	Strategic Metrics
754	Management Metrics
755	Tactical Metrics
756	Operational Metrics
757	Metametrics
758	The Business Model for Information Security, or BMIS
759	System Theory
760	Systems Thinking
761	Organization
762	Design
763	Information
764	Knowledge
765	Data
766	Enterprise Governance

767	Term: A process that sets the strategic direction of a business by defining goals
768	Term: A process that is concerned with both business goals and how a business operates internally
769	Term: A process that is concerned with all things IT
770	Term: The trifecta of governance, risk management and compliance
771	Term: The action of addressing known risks until they are at acceptable levels, identifying potential risks and associated impacts, and prioritizing both against our business goals
772	Term: The act of reducing risk
773	Term: The act of measuring policies, procedures and controls to ensure they are being enacted and effective
774	Term: A measure of the impact if we lose control of information
775	Term: A measure of the impact if we accidentally disclose information
776	Term: A collective made up of senior representatives from all impacted groups
777	Term: Those who must exercise due care and is ultimately responsible for ensuring sufficient resources are made available to address security risk
778	Term: The person in charge of enterprise risk management
779	Term: The person who handles IT planning, budgeting and performance
780	Term: The person who performs the same functions as the security manager, but holds greater authority and reports to the CEO, COO or the board of directors
781	Term: The person who is responsible for security programs creating a methodology to identify and manage risk, usually including IT systems
782	Term: The people who ensure controls are in place to address CIA, and who must approve changes to IT systems
783	Term: The managers responsible for business operations and the IT procurement processes
784	Term: The people who interact with IT systems on a daily basis and enact changes as needed
785	Term: The people who understand risk management goals and processes and create training materials and programs to spread this knowledge to the appropriate employees

767	Corporate Governance
768	Information Security Governance
769	IT Governance
770	GRC
771	Risk Management
772	Mitigation
773	Compliance
774	Criticality
775	Sensitivity
776	Steering Committee
777	Governing Board and Senior Management
778	Chief Risk Officer, or CRO
779	Chief Information Officer, or CIO
780	Chief Information Security Officer, or CISO
781	Information Security Manager
782	System and Information Owners
783	Business and Functional Managers
784	IT Security Practitioners
785	Security Awareness Trainers

786	Term: The combination of physical and information security
787	Term: Another name for convergence
788	Term: Built-in decision points that force a review to make sure a business case is still valid
789	Term: Another name for a stage gate
790	Term: A foundation on top of which multiple architectures can be built
791	Term: The architecture that is to be built
792	Term: The foundation on top of which the entire company is built
793	Term: A subset of enterprise architecture designed to give a jump-start on designing an information security program
794	Term: An activity used to determine information security deficiencies in terms of controls and compliancy
795	Term: Insurance that covers the organization from most sources and includes business interruption, direct loss and recovery costs
796	Term: Insurance that covers liability with third-parties such as defense against lawsuits and damages
797	Term: Insurance that protects against employee or agent theft and embezzlement
798	Term: The location and delivery of information in response to a request in which the company is legally bound to comply with
799	Term: A standard that has not seen wide-spread acceptance and is currently being rewritten
800	Term: An organization that released a document in 2010 called The CIS Security Metrics based on the consensus of 150 industry professionals
801	Term: A standard that aligns with the security controls listed in NIST SP 800-53
802	Term: Occurs when the investment in security provides the greatest support for business goals
803	Term: The processes to plan, allocate and control resources
804	Term: Occurs when information security lines up with our business strategy
805	Term: The act of striking the right balance between taking advantage of opportunities for gain while minimizing the chances of loss
806	Term: A phase of risk assessment where we create a list of vulnerabilities and take inventory of current threats

786	Convergence
787	Assurance Integration
788	Stage Gates
789	Kill Point
790	Architecture Framework
791	Reference Architecture
792	Enterprise Architecture Represents
793	Enterprise Information Security Architecture, or EISA
794	Audit
795	First-Party Insurance
796	Third-Party Insurance
797	Fidelity Insurance
798	E-discovery
799	ISO 27004
800	The Center for Internet Security, or CIS
801	NIST SP 800-55
802	Value Delivery
803	Information Security Resource Management
804	Strategically Alignment
805	Risk Management
806	Risk Identification Phase

807	Term: A phase of risk assessment where we take each risk and perform a BIA to come up with the possible impact
808	Term: A phase of risk assessment where we look at the impact from each risk and decide if it falls within an acceptable range based on our risk appetite, tolerance and capacity.
809	Term: The act of making sure that an organization's security policies, standards and procedures are being followed
810	Term: A procedure that makes sure another procedure is being followed
811	Term: A means for business units or departments to request an exception to an existing policy
812	Term: A process that looks at all business functions, and for the most important figures out what resources are critical for that function to continue operating
813	Term: A contract clause allowing the customer to initiate an audit given sufficient notice to the vendor
814	Term: A contract clause requiring little or no advanced notice of an inspection
815	Term: The plan to achieve risk management goals
816	Term: Achieving defined goals by bringing together human, physical and financial resources to make the best decisions
817	Term: A department that oversees all projects
818	Term: Occurs when a specific threat affects a large number of minor vulnerabilities
819	Term: Occurs when a single failure leads to a chain reaction of other failures
820	Term: An approach that allows us to decompose risk and understand the underlying components
821	Term: A methodology to look at complex life cycles from concept to retirement
822	Term: The act of determining the type and nature of viable threats, and which vulnerabilities might be exploited by each threat

807	Risk Analysis Phase
808	Risk Evaluation Phase
809	Compliance Enforcement
810	Enforcement Procedure
811	Policy Exception
812	Business Resource Dependency Assessment
813	Right-To-Audit
814	Right-To-Inspect
815	Risk Management Strategy
816	Management
817	Project Management Office, or PMO
818	Aggregated Risk
819	Cascading Risk
820	Factor Analysis of Information Risk, or FAIR
821	Probabilistic Risk Assessment, or PRA
822	Risk Identification

823	Term: The potential loss when a vulnerability is exploited by a threat
824	Term: Represents a negative event affecting a large part of the area or industry
825	Term: Occurs when multiple failures happen within a very short time frame of each other
826	Term: The minimum security level across the entire organization
827	Term: Finding the root cause of an emerging issue
828	Term: The operational component of incident management
829	Term: An incident response team that deals with fires and other emergency scenarios
830	Term: An incident response team that assesses the physical damage and decides what is a total loss or can be salvaged
831	Term: An incident response team that moves operations from the affected site to an alternate site, and then back once the original site has been restored
832	Term: An incident response team that takes care of all security concerns, including monitoring the security of systems and communications
833	Term: An incident response team that coordinates the activities of all other teams and makes the key decisions
834	Term: A report that uses color to quickly convey status
835	Term: All activities and resources that provide information security services to an organization
836	Term: Compliance in which external regulations and legislation demand compliance
837	Term: Compliance where we are obligated by a contract to remain in compliance
838	Term: Compliance in which we impose self-constraints for our own benefit
839	Term: An individual or group that helps us to identify and manage risk in a specific area, as well as monitor the effectiveness of mitigation controls in that area.
840	Term: A service that covers all processes or tasks associated with handling events and incidents
841	Term: Ensures that incidents are detected, recorded and managed to limit impacts

823	Exposure
824	Systemic Risk
825	Contagious Risk
826	Baseline Security
827	Problem Management
828	Incident Response Plan, or IRP
829	Emergency Action Team
830	Damage Assessment Team
831	Relocation Team
832	Security Team
833	Emergency Management Team
834	Red-Amber-Green Report
835	Information Security Program
836	Statutory Compliance
837	Contractual Compliance
838	Internal Compliance
839	Assurance Provider
840	Incident Handling
841	Incident Management

842	Term: The last step in handling an incident, and carries out mitigation, containment, and recovery
843	Term: An incident response team model in which we have only one team
844	Term: An incident response team model that supports multiple teams, each responsible for a different logical or physical segment of the infrastructure
845	Term: An incident response team model in in which we have multiple distributed teams that manage and implement responses but rely upon a single central team providing all guidance and policy decisions
846	Term: An incident response team model in we simply outsource at least a portion of the security team
847	Term: A tool that gathers logs from across the network and combines the data into a single database

842	Incident Response
843	Central IRT Model
844	Distributed IRT Model
845	Coordinating IRT Model
846	Outsourced IRT Model
847	Security Information and Event Manager, or SIEM

Section 2

This section contains the same terms, definitions and questions that were covered in Section 1, but in a random order. This will make it more difficult for you to infer the correct answer based on previous prompts. If you can answer all content in this section quickly and confidently, then you are very close to being ready to sit for the exam.

Why only 'close'? That was for those of you who thought you could get away without reading the Exam Guide book and skip right to the quiz. You must understand the concepts, not just memorize them if you want to pass the exam!

Section 2

1	Term: A high-level statement of what senior management expects and will dictate the direction in which we are heading
2	Define: Compliance
3	What three locations should have a copy of the recovery plan?
4	Term: The behavior of a control when a failure is encountered and locks down all access
5	Term: The behavior of a control when a failure is encountered and behaves as if the control were never in-place to begin with
6	Define: Fidelity Insurance
7	Define: Guideline
8	Define: Qualitative Analysis
9	What are the four different areas of governance?
10	Term: An organization providing quite a number of standards and frameworks, most notably NIST 800-30 and NIST 800-39
11	Define: Exposure
12	Define: Principle of Least Privilege
13	Term: A measurement taken after a reference point later and is used to see how far off we are, or how far we have come
14	What are the three control methods?
15	Term: Any control that is not a countermeasure.
16	Define: Frameworks
17	Define: Key Performance Indicator, or KPI
18	Term: A US federal law passed in 1996 to protect the privacy of a patient's medical information

Section 2

115

1	Policy
2	The act of measuring policies, procedures and controls to ensure they are being enacted and effective
3	The recovery site, a media storage facility, and at the homes of key decision-makers
4	Fail Secure
5	Fail Unsecure
6	Insurance that protects against employee or agent theft and embezzlement
7	Put into effect to reduce risk
8	A risk approach in which the magnitude of the impact and likelihood of the potential consequences are arranged on a 2-dimensional matrix
9	<ul><li>Enterprise</li><li>Corporate</li><li>IT</li><li>Information Security</li></ul>
10	The US National Institute of Standards and Technology, or NIST
11	The potential loss when a vulnerability is exploited by a threat
12	An approach that segments all resources so that we can increase access as-needed
13	Measured Point
14	<ul><li>Physical</li><li>Technical</li><li>Procedural</li></ul>
15	General Control
16	An architectural category which are very flexible and open
17	A value that tells us how well a process is performing relative to reaching a goal
18	The Health Insurance Portability and Accountability Act, or HIPAA

Section 2

19	Define: Applications Architecture Domain
20	Define: Operational Metrics
21	Term: A security mechanism that prevents a single role from having too much power
22	Term: Freedom from unwanted intrusion or disclosure of information.
23	Define: Enterprise Information Security Architecture (EISA)
24	Term: A process that watches over the entire organization or business
25	Define: Compartmentalize to Minimize Damage
26	Term: The recovery of IT systems after a disruption
27	Define: Reference Architecture
28	Define: Business Interruption Insurance
29	Define: Kill Point
30	Term: Prevents unauthorized disclosure of information
31	Term: Relevant to security means that we trust an external party to tell us if a user's identity has been authenticated and is valid
32	Define: Privacy
33	Term: Data having meaning and purpose
34	Define: Risk Management
35	Term: The act of determining the type and nature of viable threats, and which vulnerabilities might be exploited by each threat
36	Define: Risk
37	Term: The TOGAF architecture domain which describes the hardware, software and networks needed to implement applications

Section 2

19	The TOGAF architecture domain which provides a blueprint for the systems to be deployed, and describes their interaction and how they relate to business processes
20	Metrics that are comprised of technical and procedural metrics such as existing vulnerabilities and the progress of our patch management processes
21	Segregation of Duties
22	Privacy
23	An architecture designed to prevent ad-hoc, haphazard network architectures that are incredibly difficult to secure
24	Enterprise Governance
25	An approach that groups resources into separate 'compartments', with each requiring a unique authorization control
26	Disaster Recovery
27	The architecture that is to be built
28	An insurance policy an organization purchases to cover itself in the event that RTO is exceeded.
29	Another name for a stage gate
30	Confidentiality
31	Trust
32	Freedom from unwanted intrusion or disclosure of information.
33	Information
34	The action of addressing known risks until they are at acceptable levels, identifying potential risks and associated impacts, and prioritizing both against our business goals
35	Risk Identification
36	The likelihood that a threat agent will exploit a vulnerability combined with the damage that could result
37	Technical Architecture Domain

Section 2

38	Term: Measures the correlation of multiple risk events
39	Term: The danger that a vulnerability might be exploited
40	Term: The people who interact with IT systems on a daily basis and enact changes as needed
41	Term: Another name for MTO
42	What are the five types of basic tests?
43	Define: Reciprocal Agreement
44	Define: Elasticity
45	Define: Interdependency
46	Define: The US National Institute of Standards and Technology, or NIST
47	Term: Occurs when a specific threat affects a large number of minor vulnerabilities
48	Define: Platform as a Service, or PaaS
49	Term: A framework created by ISACA and is geared specifically to IT
50	Define: Cloud Computing
51	What are the five steps in incident management to effectively handle incidents?
52	What three things do audit 'work papers' accomplish?

Section 2

38	Interdependency
39	Threat
40	IT Security Practitioners
41	Maximum Tolerable Downtime, or MTD
42	• checklist review • Structured walkthrough • Simulation • Parallel • Full interruption
43	An agreement between one or more businesses that promise to share their data centers and systems in the event one of the partners experiences an outage
44	Occurs when resource can rapidly scale up or down in response to real-time business needs
45	Measures the correlation of multiple risk events
46	An organization providing quite a number of standards and frameworks, most notably NIST 800-30 and NIST 800-39
47	Aggregated Risk
48	A cloud-based offering that manages operating systems, middleware and other run-time components
49	The Control Objectives for Information and Related Technologies, or COBIT
50	An approach to hosting applications somewhere in "the cloud" as opposed to being in a known location
51	• Planning and preparation • Detection, triage and investigation • Containment, analysis, tracking and recovery • Post-incident assessment • Incident closure
52	• Maps controls to objectives • Describes what the team did to test those controls • Links the test results to the final assessment of effectiveness

Section 2

120

53	Define: Information Security Governance
54	Term: Another name for management metrics
55	Define: Risk Register
56	Define: Sensitivity
57	Define: Clustering
58	What two factors dictate the overall strength of a control?
59	Define: First-Party Insurance
60	Term: A way to create a computer in-memory, such that multiple virtual computers are running simultaneously on one physical computer
61	Term: The minimum level of service that must be restored after an event until normal operations can be resumed
62	What are the 5 views that both the SABSA and Zachman frameworks use?
63	Term: Occurs when information security lines up with our business strategy
64	Term: A phase of risk assessment where we create a list of vulnerabilities and take inventory of current threats
65	What are 5 non-framework approaches used for developing and implementing a strategy?
66	Term: A firewall that links two networks together
67	Term: A self-contained network that provides mass storage using any number of internal media such as hard drives, optical disks or tape drives

53	A process that is concerned with both business goals and how a business operates internally
54	Tactical Metrics
55	A central list of all information security risks including specific threats, vulnerabilities, exposures and assets
56	The impact that unauthorized disclosure of an asset will have
57	Another name for load balancing
58	- Inherent strength - Likelihood the control will be effective
59	Insurance that covers the organization from most sources and includes business interruption, direct loss and recovery costs
60	Virtualization
61	Service Delivery Objective, or SDO
62	- Contextual - Conceptual - Logical - Physical - Organizational
63	Strategically Alignment
64	Risk Identification Phase
65	- ISO 9001 - Six Sigma - NIST publications - Information Security Forum (ISF) publications - US Federal Information Security Modernization Act (FISMA)
66	Gateway
67	Storage Area Network, or SAN

Section 2

68	Define: Public Cloud
69	If a procedural task is preferred, what term should we use?
70	Define: Fail Unsecure
71	Define: Strategic Metrics
72	Term: The number of times a threat on a single asset is expected to happen in a single year
73	What are the four categories of resources?
74	Define: Risk Capacity
75	What are the three categories that compliance requirements fall into?
76	Define: Probability
77	Define: Risk Analysis
78	Term: A process that is concerned with both business goals and how a business operates internally
79	What are the three most common ways to find out what capability we have for reporting incidents?
80	Term: A storage device that is a self-contained server, usually running some flavor of Linux, and is accessed through a network connection
81	Term: Mechanisms, processes and systems that are available for use
82	What six attributes can be used to characterize a risk?

68	An application hosted across the Internet and publicly accessible
69	'Should'
70	The behavior of a control when a failure is encountered and behaves as if the control were never in-place to begin with
71	Metrics that provide the information necessary to guide decisions at the senior management level
72	Annualized Rate of Occurrence, or ARO
73	<ul><li>Human</li><li>Financial</li><li>Technical</li><li>Knowledge</li></ul>
74	The amount of risk a business can absorb without ceasing to exist
75	<ul><li>Statutory compliance</li><li>Contractual compliance</li><li>Internal compliance</li></ul>
76	The likelihood that a threat will exploit a vulnerability
77	The act of identifying the level for a risk, understanding its nature, and determining potential consequences
78	Information Security Governance
79	<ul><li>Surveys</li><li>Using a self-assessment</li><li>Using an external assessment or audit</li></ul>
80	Network Attached Storage, or NAS
81	Resources
82	<ul><li>Origin</li><li>Threat</li><li>Impact</li><li>Specific reason for its occurrence</li><li>Exposure and controls</li><li>Time and place of occurrence</li></ul>

Section 2

83	Term: An approach that allows us to decompose risk and understand the underlying components
84	Term: Another name for convergence
85	Define: Sensitivity
86	Define: Biased Evaluation
87	What five teams are referenced by the incident response plan?
88	Term: The processes to plan, allocate and control resources
89	What four attributes must a process possess to be of value?
90	Term: A network continuity method that routes information through an alternate medium such as copper cable or fiber optics
91	Term: A description of something that a person with that role is expected to accomplish
92	Define: Critical Success Factor, or CSF
93	Define: Reference Point
94	What are four factors to consider when deciding on the type of site to be used for recovery operations?
95	Define: Velocity

Section 2

83	Factor Analysis of Information Risk, or FAIR
84	Assurance Integration
85	A measure of the impact if we accidentally disclose information
86	Similar to Biased Assimilation, but we go one step further and attack anyone presenting facts that conflict with our own
87	- Emergency action team - Damage assessment team - Relocation team - Security team - Emergency management team
88	Information Security Resource Management
89	- Meet some type of business requirements - Be adaptable to changing requirements. - Be well documented - Be reviewed periodically
90	Alternative Routing
91	Responsibility
92	An element or event that must occur if we are to reach a KGI
93	Some type of a baseline represented by a known value taken at some point in the past
94	- AIW, RTO, RPO, SDO and MTO - The distance to potential hazards - The distance between the primary and alternate sites - The nature of probable disruptions
95	Measures two intervals - the amount of time from warning to the actual event, and the time from the actual event and subsequent impact

Section 2

96	Define: Problem Management
97	Define: Residual Risk
98	How often should plans be tested?
99	Define: Logical Control
100	Term: A control that stops attempts to violate a security policy, such as access control, encryption or authentication
101	Term: A private cloud that a select few other companies can access
102	Term: Insurance that covers the organization from most sources and includes business interruption, direct loss and recovery costs
103	Term: A cloud-based offering providing forensic tools and expertise
104	Define: One-Way Hash
105	Term: A contract clause requiring little or no advanced notice of an inspection
106	Which security access control allows anyone with access to a resource to pass that access on to other users at their 'discretion'?
107	Define: Assurance Integration
108	Term: A network continuity method that provides redundancy for voice lines
109	Which is more effective - a countermeasure or general control?
110	Term: Tools that provide an easy and comprehensive way to secure the path between a company and hosted cloud services
111	What three techniques does risk analysis include?
112	Define: Posttest Phase
113	What are the five key principles that COBIT is based on?

Section 2

96	Finding the root cause of an emerging issue
97	The amount of risk left over after it has been mitigated
98	At least once each year
99	Another name for a technical control
100	Preventative Control
101	Community Cloud
102	First-Party Insurance
103	Forensics as a Service, or FRaaS
104	Used primarily to encrypt passwords in a way that is unencryptable
105	Right-To-Inspect
106	DAC
107	Another name for convergence
108	Voice Recovery
109	A countermeasure
110	Cloud Access Security Brokers, or CASBs
111	<ul><li>Interviews</li><li>Simulations</li><li>Analysis</li></ul>
112	The plan test phase which cleans up after the test by returning people and assets to their correct location, disconnecting test equipment, and deleting company data from all third-party systems
113	<ul><li>Meeting stakeholder needs</li><li>Covering the enterprise end-to-end</li><li>Applying a single, integrated framework</li><li>Enabling a holistic approach</li><li>Separating governance from management</li></ul>

Section 2

114	Define: Process Models
115	Term: Being able to manage security risks by keeping vulnerabilities and threats to a level that we can live with
116	Define: Network Attached Storage, or NAS
117	Define: Professional and Commercial Liability Insurance
118	What are the five steps defined in CMU/SEI's Defining Incident Management Processes?
119	Term: A phase of risk assessment where we take each risk and perform a BIA to come up with the possible impact
120	Define: Bow Tie Analysis
121	Define: Man-Made Threat
122	What two attributes represent the business value of information assets?
123	Term: Built-in decision points that force a review to make sure a business case is still valid
124	Term: Occurs when an organization decides that no action is required for a specific risk
125	Term: Created by comparing two data points to each other
126	Define: Information Technology Infrastructure Library, or ITIL
127	Define: Disaster Recovery as a Service, or DRaaS
128	Define: Distributed IRT Model
129	Define: Management Metrics

Section 2

129	
114	An architectural category which dictates the processes used for each element
115	Assurance
116	A storage device that is a self-contained server, usually running some flavor of Linux, and is accessed through a network connection
117	Insurance which protects a business from losses experienced as a result of third-party claims.
118	<ul><li>Prepare</li><li>Protect</li><li>Detect</li><li>Triage</li><li>Respond</li></ul>
119	Risk Analysis Phase
120	A risk approach that creates a visual diagram with the cause of an event in the middle, representing the 'knot' of a bow tie, with triggers, controls and consequences branching off of the 'knot'.
121	A type of threat that results from man-made actions
122	Sensitivity and criticality
123	Stage Gates
124	Risk Acceptance
125	Metric
126	A set of detailed practices for managing IT services with a special focus on aligning those services with the needs of business
127	A cloud-based offering taking on the responsibility of hosting and maintaining a disaster recovery solution
128	An incident response team model that supports multiple teams, each responsible for a different logical or physical segment of the infrastructure
129	Metrics that is used by the security manager to determine if the security program is remaining in compliance, is tackling emerging risk and is in alignment with business goals

130	Term: The result we want to achieve
131	Define: PKI
132	What are the four primary elements in BMIS?
133	Define: Project Management Office, or PMO
134	Which is more efficient in terms of coverage - a countermeasure or general control?
135	Term: Factors that work against efficiency
136	Term: Caused when a threat exploits a vulnerability and causes a loss
137	Define: Information Security Manager
138	Term: The plan test phase which cleans up after the test by returning people and assets to their correct location, disconnecting test equipment, and deleting company data from all third-party systems
139	Define: Cold Site
140	Define: ISACA
141	Term: A risk approach where we use categories to represent levels of risk using a numerical value
142	Term: A control deployed to counter a specific threat known to exist
143	Term: Factors that individually or collectively influence whether something will work
144	Term: A framework that helps organizations reach an elevated level of performance
145	Define: Security Information and Event Manager, or SIEM
146	Term: A control capable of providing warnings that can deter a potential compromise
147	Define: Full Operational Test

Section 2

131

130	Goal
131	Public key infrastructure; how SSL and TLS certificates work invisibly
132	- Organization - People - Process - Technology
133	A department that oversees all projects
134	A general control
135	Constraints
136	Impact
137	The person who is responsible for security programs creating a methodology to identify and manage risk, usually including IT systems
138	Posttest Phase
139	A recovery site that only provides the basic infrastructure with no servers or software, and can take up to multiple weeks to bring online
140	An organization who owns the CISM certification, and who has created the Risk IT Framework.
141	Semiquantitative Analysis
142	Countermeasure
143	COBIT 5 Enabler
144	Capability Maturity Model Integration, or CMMI
145	A tool that gathers logs from across the network and combines the data into a single database
146	Deterrent Control
147	A plan test category which is the same as a full interruption test

148	Define: Mandatory access control, or MAC
149	Define: Right-To-Audit
150	Term: A term used to describe a central command point from which all other activities are directed
151	What are the three things that all architecture frameworks seek to do?
152	What are the seven categories of COBIT 5 enablers?
153	Term: An analysis that helps us to understand what assets are important, and what their loss will mean to us
154	What four things is the acceptable level of risk based on?
155	Define: Recovery Site
156	Term: A risk approach that is great when we need a well-established process to identify, prioritize and manage risk
157	Define: Segregation of Duties
158	Term: A network device that limits traffic to certain IP addresses and ports
159	What are the three types of threats?
160	Term: A central list of all information security risks including specific threats, vulnerabilities, exposures and assets

Section 2

133

148	A security access control that looks at the classification of the requested resource and compares it to the security clearance of the user
149	A contract clause allowing the customer to initiate an audit given sufficient notice to the vendor
150	Command and Control (C&C)
151	• Detail the roles, entities and relationships that exist • Provide a taxonomy (naming conventions) for all processes that describes how they are executed and secured • Deliver a set of artifacts describing how a business operates and what security controls are required
152	• Principles, policies and frameworks • Processes • Organizational structures • Culture, ethics and behavior • Information • Services, infrastructure and applications • People, skills and competencies
153	Business Impact Analysis, or BIA
154	• The ability to absorb loss • The risk appetite • The cost to achieve acceptable risk levels • Risk/benefit ratios
155	A location where we move operations after the original site has been compromised
156	Operationally Critical Threat Asset and Vulnerability Evaluation, or OCTAVE
157	A security mechanism that prevents a single role from having too much power
158	Firewall
159	Natural, manmade or technical
160	Risk Register

Section 2

161	What three things does information systems architecture consider?
162	Define: Systems Thinking
163	Define: Simulation Test
164	Define: Intrusion Detection System, or IDS
165	Define: Forensics as a Service, or FRaaS
166	Define: Vulnerability
167	Define: Business Continuity
168	What are the three types of insurance?
169	Term: An approach that views a system as a complete functioning unit - not simply the sum of its parts
170	Term: A cloud-based offering that is an application that someone hosts and maintains.
171	Define: Mitigation
172	Term: A standard that aligns with the security controls listed in NIST SP 800-53
173	Define: Architecture Framework
174	Term: Part of the ISO 27000 series that provides best practices for information security controls
175	Term: A data storage device that is connected directly to a server or client
176	Term: Where we are now
177	Define: IT Governance
178	Term: An organization that owns multiple other security certifications, such as the CISSP.
179	When coming into a new environment, what is the best approach to get a handle on what needs to be done?

Section 2

135

161	• Goals • Environment • Technical skills
162	A thought method that drives us to study the results of interactions within a system
163	A plan test in which team members role-play a simulated disaster without activating the recovery site
164	A network device that looks for patterns indicative of an attack and sends out alerts
165	A cloud-based offering providing forensic tools and expertise
166	A weakness in a system that allows a threat to compromise security
167	A strategy to prevent, recover and continue from disasters
168	• First-Party • Third-Party • Fidelity
169	System Theory
170	Software as a Service, or SaaS
171	The act of reducing risk
172	NIST SP 800-55
173	A foundation on top of which multiple architectures can be built
174	ISO 27002
175	Direct Attached Storage, or DAS
176	Current State
177	A process that is concerned with all things IT
178	The International Information Systems Security Certification Consortium, Inc., or (ISC)2
179	To first understand what those above expect, followed with an abundance of documentation on those expectations.

Section 2

136

180	Define: Risk Identification Phase
181	Term: The TOGAF architecture domain which provides a blueprint for the systems to be deployed, and describes their interaction and how they relate to business processes
182	What are the five steps involved in problem management?
183	Term: A situation in which we cannot deny having sent a message
184	Define: Pretest Phase
185	Term: The TOGAF architecture domain which defines the business strategy, governance, organization and key business processes
186	Term: The amount of time normal operations can be down before the organization faces major financial problems that threaten its existence
187	What are the five phases of the system development life cycle, or SDLC?
188	Term: An approach to hosting applications somewhere in 'the cloud' as opposed to being in a known location
189	Define: Internal Compliance
190	Define: RACI Chart
191	What are the four options for addressing risk?

Section 2

137

180	A phase of risk assessment where we create a list of vulnerabilities and take inventory of current threats
181	Applications Architecture Domain
182	- Understanding the issue - Defining the problem - Designing an action program - Assigning responsibility - Assigning due dates for resolution
183	Nonrepudiation
184	The plan test phase which sets the stage for the actual test
185	Business Architecture Domain
186	Allowable Interruption Window, or AIW
187	- Initiation - Development and acquisition - Implementation - Operation or maintenance - Disposal
188	Cloud Computing
189	Compliance in which we impose self-constraints for our own benefit
190	A 2-dimensional matrix that lists roles on one axis, and responsibilities on another axis
191	- Accept - Mitigate - Avoid - Transfer

Section 2

192	If a procedural task is mandatory, what terms should we use?
193	Term: A measure of the impact if we lose control of information
194	Term: A recovery site that has the complete infrastructure ready to go, but usually is not able to operate at the capacity of the original site
195	Define: Emergency Management Team
196	Define: Fault Tree Analysis
197	Term: Insurance which protects a business from losses experienced as a result of third-party claims.
198	Define: Cybersecurity Insurance
199	What three steps are required when measuring success?
200	Define: Gateway
201	For value at risk, or VAR, to be useful, what do we have to have a lot of?
202	Term: The act of measuring policies, procedures and controls to ensure they are being enacted and effective
203	What are four types of third-parties entities?
204	Term: Achieving defined goals by bringing together human, physical and financial resources to make the best decisions
205	What are the four steps of the risk management life cycle?

Section 2

139

192	'Must' and 'shall'
193	Criticality
194	Warm Site
195	An incident response team that coordinates the activities of all other teams and makes the key decisions
196	A risk approach that is a top-down model where we start with an event and look for possible causes for that event to occur
197	Professional and Commercial Liability Insurance
198	Insurance that covers losses incurred as a result of a cyberattack
199	<ul><li>Defining measurable goals</li><li>Tracking the most appropriate metrics</li><li>Periodically analyzing those results so we know where to make adjustments</li></ul>
200	A firewall that links two networks together
201	Historical data that is very accurate
202	Compliance
203	<ul><li>Service providers</li><li>Outsourced operations</li><li>Trading partners</li><li>Merged or acquired organizations</li></ul>
204	Management
205	<ul><li>IT risk identification</li><li>IT risk assessment</li><li>Risk response and mitigation</li><li>Risk and control monitoring and reporting</li></ul>

Section 2

206	What are the six common methods for ensuring continuity of network services?
207	Term: The people who ensure controls are in place to address CIA, and who must approve changes to IT systems
208	Term: A foundation on top of which multiple architectures can be built
209	Define: Assurance Provider
210	Define: Federated Identity
211	Define: Technical Architecture Domain
212	Define: Proximity
213	Term: Occurs when a vulnerability is taken advantage of by an attacker
214	Term: The impact that unauthorized disclosure of an asset will have
215	Term: The maximum amount of time allowed to return compromised facilities and systems back to an acceptable level of operation
216	Define: Redundancy
217	Term: The amount of data we can stand to permanently lose in case of interruption in terms of time, usually hours or days.
218	What are the six steps in a typical APT attack?
219	Term: Another name for a procedural control

206	• Redundancy • Alternative routing • Diverse routing • Long-haul network diversity • Last-mile circuit protection • Voice recovery
207	System and Information Owners
208	Architecture Framework
209	An individual or group that helps us to identify and manage risk in a specific area, as well as monitor the effectiveness of mitigation controls in that area.
210	An identity solution when identity access management itself is hosted in the cloud
211	The TOGAF architecture domain which describes the hardware, software and networks needed to implement applications
212	Indicates the time between an event and impact
213	Exploit
214	Sensitivity
215	Recovery Time Objective, or RTO
216	A network continuity method in which we provide fail-over systems
217	Recovery Point Objective, or RPO
218	• Initial compromise • Establish foothold • Escalate privileges • Internal reconnaissance • Move laterally • Maintain presence • Complete the mission
219	Administrative Control

Section 2

142

220	Term: A phase of risk assessment where we look at the impact from each risk and decide if it falls within an acceptable range based on our risk appetite, tolerance and capacity.
221	What is the disadvantage of using a quantitative approach to assessing impact?
222	What are the seven phases typically included in BCP planning?
223	Term: A risk prior to mitigation.
224	Define: Emerging Threat
225	What are the two primary benefits of an SIEM?
226	What are two reasons that the security team possess some programming skills?
227	Why is a centralized information security approach the preferred method?
228	Term: A plan test in which the recovery site is brought up to a state of operational readiness, but operations at the primary site continue
229	What are the two types of outsourcing a security manager will have to deal with?
230	Define: Knowledge
231	Term: A cloud-based offering that hosts and analyzes big data, requiring you to only ask a question
232	Define: Operationally Critical Threat Asset and Vulnerability Evaluation, or OCTAVE

220	Risk Evaluation Phase
221	The quantitative meanings may be unclear, requiring a qualitative explanation
222	- Conducting a risk assessment or a BIA - Defining a response and recovery strategy - Documenting response and recovery plans - Training that covers response and recovery procedures - Updating response and recovery plans - Testing response and recovery plans - Auditing response and recovery plans
223	Inherent Risk
224	Mounting evidence that something nefarious is going on in the organization's network and systems
225	- Lower operating costs - Decreased response times to an event
226	- To be able to detect vulnerabilities - To be able to coach developers on secure coding practices
227	It provides the best alignment across all business units
228	Parallel Test
229	- Third-parties providing security services - Outsourced IT or business processes that must be integrated into the information security program
230	Information that has been absorbed
231	Information as a Service, or IaaS
232	A risk approach that is great when we need a well-established process to identify, prioritize and manage risk

Section 2

233	Define: Support Control
234	Define: Skill
235	Define: Authenticate
236	What are the processes involved with risk management?
237	What is the BMIS dynamic relationship between Process and Technology?
238	Term: An application hosted across the Internet and publicly accessible
239	Define: Storage Area Network, or SAN
240	What four things must a metric do to have true value?
241	What are two tools that help with selection of a cloud service provider?
242	Term: An approach where higher-level goals define what the different enablers should achieve
243	Define: Access Control
244	Define: Confirmation Bias
245	Define: Discretionary access control, or DAC
246	What four functions does incident handling involve?

145	
233	A control technology category representing technologies that automate a security-related procedure, process management information or increase management capabilities
234	The training, expertise and experience an individual has for a given role
235	Proving identity by providing something a person is, has or knows
236	• establish scope and boundaries, • identify information assets and valuation • perform the risk assessment, • determine risk treatment or response • accept residual risk, • communicate about and monitor risk.
237	Enabling and Support
238	Public Cloud
239	A self-contained network that provides mass storage using any number of internal media such as hard drives, optical disks or tape drives
240	• Deliver whatever is important to manage information security operations • Meet IT security management requirements • Meet the needs of business process owners • Provide what senior management wants to know
241	CSA Cloud Control Matrix and the Jericho Forum Self-Assessment Scheme
242	COBIT 5 Goals Cascade
243	The act of controlling who has access to sensitive information based on their identity
244	Occurs when we seek opinions and facts that support a conclusion we have already reached
245	A security access control using groups to make security administration easier
246	• Detection and reporting • Triage • Analysis • Incident response

247	What three things must we accomplish to be strategically aligned?
248	What four aspects should be considered for each threat evaluated?
249	Term: A fault-tolerant configuration in which both the primary and fail-over systems process load during normal use, and on failure of either system the remaining system takes on all load.
250	Define: COBIT 5 Goals Cascade
251	Define: Hot Site
252	Term: Shown when we purposefully try and discover things that can go wrong
253	Define: Governing Board and Senior Management
254	Define: Errors and Omissions Insurance
255	Term: A plan test in which that activates the recovery site and shuts down the primary site.
256	Term: The plan to achieve risk management goals
257	Define: The International Information Systems Security Certification Consortium, Inc., or (ISC)2
258	Define: Countermeasure
259	Define: The International Organization for Standardization, or ISO
260	Term: A procedure that makes sure another procedure is being followed

147

247	- The enterprise defines what good security looks like. - Security matches the company's DNA instead of trying to rewrite it. - The amount of money we spend on security accurately reflects how important security is to us.
248	- If it is real - How likely it is to happen - How large the impact might be - Which systems, operations, personnel and facilities will be affected
249	Load Balancing
250	An approach where higher-level goals define what the different enablers should achieve
251	A recovery site that is fully configured and can be ready to operate in a number of hours
252	Due Diligence
253	Those who must exercise due care and is ultimately responsible for ensuring sufficient resources are made available to address security risk
254	Insurance that legally protects a business in case it commits an act, error or omission that results in a loss
255	Full Interruption Test
256	Risk Management Strategy
257	An organization that owns multiple other security certifications, such as the CISSP.
258	A control deployed to counter a specific threat known to exist
259	An organization authoring the ISO 2000 series, of which ISO 27001 and ISO 27002 are ones the most frequently used
260	Enforcement Procedure

Section 2

261	Define: Contagious Risk
262	Define: Goal
263	Define: Nonrepudiation
264	What are the five control categories?
265	Define: Spyware
266	Term: A process that is concerned with all things IT
267	Define: Threat
268	Term: A weakness that is so new a fix is not yet available
269	Term: An incident response team that takes care of all security concerns, including monitoring the security of systems and communications
270	Define: Chief Risk Officer, or CRO
271	What is the first step to mitigate internal threats?
272	Define: Statutory Compliance
273	Term: A 2-dimensional matrix that lists roles on one axis, and responsibilities on another axis
274	What are 5 attributes a good policy will possess?
275	Define: Policy Exception

Section 2

149

261	Occurs when multiple failures happen within a very short time frame of each other
262	The result we want to achieve
263	A situation in which we cannot deny having sent a message
264	- Preventative - Detective - Corrective - Compensating - Deterrent
265	A form of malware but specifically watches whatever the user does, usually to steal credentials
266	IT Governance
267	The danger that a vulnerability might be exploited
268	Zero-Day Vulnerability
269	Security Team
270	The person in charge of enterprise risk management
271	The hiring process itself by reviewing references and background checks
272	Compliance in which external regulations and legislation demand compliance
273	RACI Chart
274	- It describes a strategy - It is a single general mandate - It is clearly and easily understood - It is only a few sentences long - It belongs to a set that is no more than two dozen in number
275	A means for business units or departments to request an exception to an existing policy

Section 2

150

276	What are 5 organizations dedicated to finding and reporting vulnerabilities?
277	Define: Resources
278	Define: Last-Mile Circuit Protection
279	Define: Authorize
280	Define: Technical Control
281	Define: Motivation
282	What are two primary aspects to consider when deciding how long to keep business records?
283	Define: Responsibility
284	Term: The act of identifying the level for a risk, understanding its nature, and determining potential consequences
285	Term: A skilled external attacker who is willing to invest considerable time and resources into bypassing an organization's network and system security controls.
286	Define: Full Interruption Test
287	What are one of the greatest sources of man-made threats?
288	What comprises the total cost of the recovery process?
289	Define: Diverse Routing
290	Term: Occurs when a private cloud connects across the public Internet into another application
291	Define: Service Delivery Objective, or SDO

276	• US Computer Emergency Readiness Team, or CERT • MITRE's Common Vulnerabilities and Exposures database • Security Focus's BUGTRAQ mailing list • The SANS Institute • OEMS
277	Mechanisms, processes and systems that are available for use
278	A network continuity method that protects the communications infrastructure connected directly to a facility
279	Deciding the level of access to resources a user should be allowed based on the authenticated identity
280	A control that always contains some type of technology whether it is hardware or software
281	Measures the type of motivation the attacker has
282	• Business requirements • Legal and regulatory requirements
283	A description of something that a person with that role is expected to accomplish
284	Risk Analysis
285	Advanced Persistent Threat (APT)
286	A plan test in which that activates the recovery site and shuts down the primary site.
287	Employees
288	• Preparing for possible disruptions before a crisis • Putting equipment and facilities into effect during a crisis • Business interruption insurance
289	A network continuity method that routes traffic through split or duplicate cables
290	Hybrid Model
291	The minimum level of service that must be restored after an event until normal operations can be resumed

Section 2

292	Term: A risk approach that looks at historical data and calculates the probability of risk
293	Define: Structured Walkthrough Test
294	Term: A weakness in a system that allows a threat to compromise security
295	Term: Compliance in which external regulations and legislation demand compliance
296	Term: A plan that documents how an organization will prevent disruptions and continue operating at a strategical level with minimal or no downtime after a serious event happens
297	Term: A title given to someone based on their job function
298	When does a decentralized information security approach works the best?
299	Define: Data
300	Term: The amount of deviation from the risk appetite a business considers acceptable
301	Define: Incident Response
302	Term: The act of making sure that an organization's security policies, standards and procedures are being followed
303	Term: Deciding the level of access to resources a user should be allowed based on the authenticated identity
304	Can we transfer financial impact of a risk?
305	What term represents the part of an organization's 'constitution'?
306	Define: Duplicate Site
307	Define: Mental Accounting Effect
308	Define: Trust
309	Define: Media Transportation Insurance

Section 2

292	Bayesian Analysis
293	A plan test in which team members implement the plan on paper
294	Vulnerability
295	Statutory Compliance
296	Business Continuity Plan, or BCP
297	Role
298	When dealing with multinational companies with locations in different countries or legal jurisdictions
299	Nothing but facts
300	Risk Tolerance
301	The last step in handling an incident, and carries out mitigation, containment, and recovery
302	Compliance Enforcement
303	Authorize
304	Yes
305	Policy
306	A recovery site configured exactly like the primary site and can be anything from a hot site to a reciprocal agreement with another company
307	Seen when we treat money differently based on where it comes from or how it is spent, and is common in boardrooms
308	Relevant to security means that we trust an external party to tell us if a user's identity has been authenticated and is valid
309	Insurance that covers loss or damage to media during transport

Section 2

310	Term: The combination of physical and information security
311	Term: Measures two intervals - the amount of time from warning to the actual event, and the time from the actual event and subsequent impact
312	Define: Risk Analysis Phase
313	Define: Recovery Time Objective, or RTO
314	Define: Exposure
315	Define: False Consensus
316	Term: The training, expertise and experience an individual has for a given role
317	Term: Something that uniquely identifies the user, such as a user name, email address or thumbprint
318	Define: Semiquantitative Analysis
319	Term: Put into effect to reduce risk
320	Define: Key Goal Indicator, or KGI
321	What three considerations must be considered when evaluating control strength?
322	Define: Information Security Program
323	Term: The plan test phase where the emergency is simulated, and people, systems and processes are moved to the recovery site to the extent the test allows
324	Define: Compliance
325	Term: A control technology category representing out-of-the-box capabilities
326	Term: An incident response team that coordinates the activities of all other teams and makes the key decisions

310	Convergence
311	Velocity
312	A phase of risk assessment where we take each risk and perform a BIA to come up with the possible impact
313	The maximum amount of time allowed to return compromised facilities and systems back to an acceptable level of operation
314	A single real-world instance of a vulnerability being exploited by a threat agent
315	The tendency to overestimate the extent to which other people share our own views or beliefs
316	Skill
317	Identity
318	A risk approach where we use categories to represent levels of risk using a numerical value
319	Control
320	A value that tells us after the fact if an IT process has achieved its goal
321	• If it is preventative or detective • If it is manual or automated • If it has formal or ad-hoc
322	All activities and resources that provide information security services to an organization
323	Test Phase
324	The act of measuring policies, procedures and controls to ensure they are being enacted and effective
325	Native Control
326	Emergency Management Team

Section 2

327	Term: Used primarily to encrypt passwords in a way that is unencryptable
328	Term: A control technology category representing technologies that automate a security-related procedure, process management information or increase management capabilities
329	What are the five steps in creating a culture?
330	Term: Occurs when we remember only facts and experiences that support our current assumptions
331	Term: Some type of a baseline represented by a known value taken at some point in the past
332	Define: The Committee of Sponsoring Organizations of the Treadway Commission, or COSO
333	Term: A recovery site that only provides the basic infrastructure with no servers or software, and can take up to multiple weeks to bring online
334	Define: ISO 27004
335	Define: Supplemental Control
336	Term: A design strategy that does not trust any one person to follow the proper procedures when administrating a system
337	Term: Metrics that is used by the security manager to determine if the security program is remaining in compliance, is tackling emerging risk and is in alignment with business goals
338	Term: The amount of risk left over after it has been mitigated
339	Define: Extra Expense Policy
340	Define: Constraints
341	Term: The person in charge of enterprise risk management

Section 2

327	One-Way Hash
328	Support Control
329	• Experience • Respond • Expected behavior • Unwritten rule • Normal
330	Selective Recall
331	Reference Point
332	An organization providing a framework called the 'COSO Framework'.
333	Cold Site
334	A standard that has not seen wide-spread acceptance and is currently being rewritten
335	A control technology category representing technology that is added to an information system after the fact
336	Trust No One
337	Management Metrics
338	Residual Risk
339	Insurance which reimburses to the business for expenses incurred in maintaining operations at a facility that experiences damage.
340	Factors that work against efficiency
341	Chief Risk Officer, or CRO

Section 2

342	Define: Aggregated Risk
343	Define: Criticality
344	What must incident management integrate with before it is of any value?
345	Term: A recovery site that is a specially designed trailer that can be quickly moved to a business location when needed
346	Term: Some type of behavior, activity or event that usually is accompanied by a rise in risk levels
347	What are the five most common sources for APTs?
348	Define: Enterprise Architecture Represents
349	Define: Herding Instinct
350	Define: Private Cloud
351	Term: An element or event that must occur if we are to reach a KGI
352	What are the four steps used to capture usable security metrics?
353	Define: Zero-Day Vulnerability
354	Define: Contractual Compliance
355	What four criteria should we look at when selecting individual KRIs?
356	Define: Management

Section 2

159

342	Occurs when a specific threat affects a large number of minor vulnerabilities
343	The impact that the loss of an asset will have, or how important the asset is to the business
344	Business processes and the BCP.
345	Mobile Site
346	Key Risk Indicator, or KRI
347	• Intelligence agencies • Criminal groups • Terrorist groups • Activist groups • Armed forces
348	The foundation on top of which the entire company is built
349	The tendency for people to 'do what everyone else is doing'
350	A network hosted entirely inside of a company's intranet and is not accessible externally.
351	Critical Success Factor, or CSF
352	• Strong Upper-Level Management Support • Practical Security Policies and Procedures • Quantifiable Performance Metrics • Results-Oriented Metrics Analysis
353	A weakness that is so new a fix is not yet available
354	Compliance where we are obligated by a contract to remain in compliance
355	• The KRI should be an indicator for risks with high impacts. • If two or more KRIs are equivalent, choose the one that is easier to measure. • The KRI must be reliable in both predicting outcomes and having a high correlation with risk. • The KRI must be able to accurately model variances in the risk level with a high degree of sensitivity.
356	Achieving defined goals by bringing together human, physical and financial resources to make the best decisions

Section 2

357	Term: The action of proving who we claim we are
358	Term: Ensures that incidents are detected, recorded and managed to limit impacts
359	Which architecture framework has enjoyed the most widespread acceptance globally?
360	Define: On-Demand Self-Service
361	What are the five factors driving convergence?
362	Define: Risk Management
363	Term: A server component designed to detect and delete email SPAM
364	Term: Metrics that provide the information necessary to guide decisions at the senior management level
365	Define: Business Recovery
366	Define: Convergence
367	Define: Audit
368	Term: A business-oriented approach to information security that models complex relationships using system theory
369	Term: Compliance in which we impose self-constraints for our own benefit
370	What one thing does a Business Resource Dependency Assessment not provide that a BIA does provide?
371	Term: The trifecta of governance, risk management and compliance
372	Term: An IDS that will actively try and stop an attack that is underway
373	Term: The TOGAF architecture domain which describes the structure of logical and physical data, and management resources
374	Term: A network continuity method in which we provide fail-over systems

Section 2

161

357	Authentication
358	Incident Management
359	COBIT 5
360	Occurs when computing capabilities are provisioned without any type of human interaction
361	• Rapid expansion of the enterprise • The increasing value of information and intangible assets above physical assets • New technologies blurring functional boundaries • New compliance and regulatory requirements • The pressure to reduce cost
362	The act of striking the right balance between taking advantage of opportunities for gain while minimizing the chances of loss
363	Antispam Device
364	Strategic Metrics
365	The recovery of all critical business processes required to resume operations
366	The combination of physical and information security
367	An activity used to determine information security deficiencies in terms of controls and compliancy
368	The Business Model for Information Security, or BMIS
369	Internal Compliance
370	The impact if resources are no longer available
371	GRC
372	Intrusion Prevention System, or IPS
373	Data Architecture Domain
374	Redundancy

Section 2

375	What are two ways in which we can get senior management support?
376	Define: Reference Models
377	Term: The operational component of incident management
378	Define: Maximum Tolerable Downtime, or MTD
379	Define: COBIT 5 Enabler
380	What are the three phases of a plan test?
381	Define: Chief Information Officer, or CIO
382	Why must care be taken with SOC 2 audits?
383	Define: Stage Gates
384	Define: Load Balancing
385	What three questions does PRA ask?
386	Define: Volatility
387	Define: Enterprise Information Security Architecture, or EISA
388	What are the three general categories of architectural approaches?
389	Define: Identity as a Service, or IDaaS

Section 2

375	• Wait for the unacceptable consequences of an incident to spur action • Create persuasive business cases detailing how similar incidents in peer organizations resulted in unacceptable consequences
376	An architectural category which are actually small-scale representations of the actual implementation
377	Incident Response Plan, or IRP
378	Another name for MTO
379	Factors that individually or collectively influence whether something will work
380	• Pretest • Test • Posttest
381	The person who handles IT planning, budgeting and performance
382	Because the outsourced provider is the one who defines the criteria
383	Built-in decision points that force a review to make sure a business case is still valid
384	A fault-tolerant configuration in which both the primary and fail-over systems process load during normal use, and on failure of either system the remaining system takes on all load.
385	• What can go wrong? • How likely is it? • What are the consequences?
386	A measure of how stable the conditions giving rise to risk are.
387	A subset of enterprise architecture designed to give a jump-start on designing an information security program
388	• Process models • Frameworks • Reference models
389	A cloud-based offering for identity management

Section 2

390	Define: Fault-Tolerant
391	What are the six components of a governance framework?
392	Term: Public key infrastructure; how SSL and TLS certificates work invisibly
393	Term: Another name for a technical control
394	Define: Third-Party Insurance
395	Term: Those who must exercise due care and is ultimately responsible for ensuring sufficient resources are made available to address security risk
396	Term: An architecture designed to prevent ad-hoc, haphazard network architectures that are incredibly difficult to secure
397	Define: Preventative Control
398	Who is the most likely to be the first to receive an incident report?
399	Define: Risk Identification
400	Term: A collective made up of senior representatives from all impacted groups
401	Define: Criticality
402	What are the five components of a security management framework?
403	Define: Metametrics
404	Define: Virtualization
405	Term: Another name for load balancing

390	A storage solution in which the primary system communicates in real-time with the fail-over system
391	- Strategy
- Policies
- Standards
- Security organization
- Workflows and structures
- A way to measure compliance
392	PKI
393	Logical Control
394	Insurance that covers liability with third-parties such as defense against lawsuits and damages
395	Governing Board and Senior Management
396	Enterprise Information Security Architecture (EISA)
397	A control that stops attempts to violate a security policy, such as access control, encryption or authentication
398	Help or service desk employees
399	The act of determining the type and nature of viable threats, and which vulnerabilities might be exploited by each threat
400	Steering Committee
401	A measure of the impact if we lose control of information
402	- Technical
- Operational
- Management
- Administrative
- Educational and Informational
403	Attributes on metrics used to calculate an overall value for prioritization
404	A way to create a computer in-memory, such that multiple virtual computers are running simultaneously on one physical computer
405	Clustering

Section 2

166

406	To provide the best chance at success, what are the three areas in which a security manager should focus?
407	The frequency of third-party usage reviews is based on what three factors?
408	Define: Capability Maturity Model Integration, or CMMI
409	Define: Sub-Policy
410	Term: A person or process that exploits a vulnerability
411	Term: The people who understand risk management goals and processes and create training materials and programs to spread this knowledge to the appropriate employees
412	Define: Balanced Scorecard
413	Define: Asset Value, or AV
414	Define: Visibility
415	Define: Business Resource Dependency Assessment
416	Define: Impact
417	What four events can cause an update to the incident response plan?
418	Term: Finding the root cause of an emerging issue
419	Define: Key Risk Indicator, or KRI
420	Define: Outsourced IRT Model
421	Term: The managers responsible for business operations and the IT procurement processes
422	Define: Business Architecture Domain

406	• Senior management support • Funding • Staffing
407	• Criticality of information • Criticality of privileges • Length of the contract
408	A framework that helps organizations reach an elevated level of performance
409	A method to address a need separate from the bulk of the organization
410	Threat agent
411	Security Awareness Trainers
412	A management system that helps organizations to create clear goals and translate them into action
413	A monetary value assigned to an asset
414	An attribute attached to the target
415	A process that looks at all business functions, and for the most important figures out what resources are critical for that function to continue operating
416	Caused when a threat exploits a vulnerability and causes a loss
417	• Organizational strategy changes • New software applications • Software or hardware environment changes • Physical and environmental changes
418	Problem Management
419	Some type of behavior, activity or event that usually is accompanied by a rise in risk levels
420	An incident response team model in we simply outsource at least a portion of the security team
421	Business and Functional Managers
422	The TOGAF architecture domain which defines the business strategy, governance, organization and key business processes

Section 2

168

423	Define: Skill
424	Define: Adware
425	Term: The amount of money we can expect to lose each year for a given risk
426	Term: Insurance that covers liability with third-parties such as defense against lawsuits and damages
427	Term: A storage solution in which the primary system communicates in real-time with the fail-over system
428	What two factors does a viable threat possess?
429	Define: Gap Analysis
430	Define: Checklist Review Test
431	Term: Occurs when we seek opinions and facts that support a conclusion we have already reached
432	Define: Router
433	What is the best indicator of how well our security program is doing?
434	What is the disadvantage of using a qualitative approach to assessing impact?
435	What five aspects should the level of security applied to hardware, software and information assets be based on?
436	Define: Endowment Effect
437	Term: A cloud-based offering that delivers storage and analysis of huge amounts of data
438	Term: An identity solution when identity access management itself is hosted in the cloud
439	Define: Current State

Section 2

423	Measures the proficiency of the attacker and informs us of potential targets
424	Unwanted software that is annoying but normally harmless
425	Annual Loss Expectancy, or ALE
426	Third-Party Insurance
427	Fault-Tolerant
428	• They exist or could reasonably appear • They can be controlled
429	An analysis of the work needed to get from the current state to the desired state
430	A plan test in which all steps are reviewed
431	Confirmation Bias
432	Allows separate networks to talk to each other by 'routing' the traffic between them
433	How much the negative impact of incidents experienced over a year exceed acceptable risk levels
434	It does not provide a measurable magnitude, making a cost-benefit analysis difficult
435	• Criticality of systems • Sensitivity of information • Significance of applications • Cost of replacement hardware • Availability of backup equipment
436	The tendency for people to hold something they already own at a higher value than if they did not already own it
437	Data Storage and Data Analytics as a Service
438	Federated Identity
439	Where we are now

Section 2

440	Define: COBIT 5 Process Assessment Model (PAM)
441	What are the six phases to develop an incident response plan?
442	Term: An individual or group that helps us to identify and manage risk in a specific area, as well as monitor the effectiveness of mitigation controls in that area.
443	Term: A network of people, assets and processes interacting with each other in defined roles and working toward a common goal
444	Term: The act of creating a plan on how a company will achieve a goal and then making sure everyone executes that plan
445	Define: Due Diligence
446	Term: A means for business units or departments to request an exception to an existing policy
447	Term: An analysis of the work needed to get from the current state to the desired state
448	Term: A thought method that drives us to study the results of interactions within a system
449	Define: The Health Insurance Portability and Accountability Act, or HIPAA
450	Term: A plan of action to achieve a goal
451	Define: Fail Secure
452	Term: The impact that the loss of an asset will have, or how important the asset is to the business
453	Term: Proving identity by providing something a person is, has or knows
454	Term: The act of reducing risk
455	Term: Nothing but facts

Section 2

440	A tool used to capture both the current and future desired state for information security
441	- Preparation - Identification - Containment - Eradication - Recovery - Lessons learned
442	Assurance Provider
443	Organization
444	Governance
445	Shown when we purposefully try and discover things that can go wrong
446	Policy Exception
447	Gap Analysis
448	Systems Thinking
449	A US federal law passed in 1996 to protect the privacy of a patient's medical information
450	Strategy
451	The behavior of a control when a failure is encountered and locks down all access
452	Criticality
453	Authenticate
454	Mitigation
455	Data

Section 2

456	What three metrics are the most useful as justification for expending resources?
457	Term: A network device that looks for patterns indicative of an attack and sends out alerts
458	How do we get from strategy to design?
459	Define: Information as a Service, or IaaS
460	In BCP, what are three strategies to proactively address threats?
461	Define: Command and Control (C&C)
462	Define: VoIP
463	Term: The person who handles IT planning, budgeting and performance
464	Term: Insurance that legally protects a business in case it commits an act, error or omission that results in a loss
465	Define: Business Continuity Plan, or BCP
466	Define: Compliance Enforcement
467	Term: A cloud-based offering that provides the customer with a ready-made network, storage and servers
468	Define: IT Security Practitioners
469	Term: A standard that has not seen wide-spread acceptance and is currently being rewritten
470	What are the three phases that OCTAVE contains?

456	- VAR - ROSI - ALE
457	Intrusion Detection System, or IDS
458	By using resources
459	A cloud-based offering that hosts and analyzes big data, requiring you to only ask a question
460	- Eliminate or neutralize a threat - Minimize the likelihood of a threat - Minimize the effects of a threat
461	A term used to describe a central command point from which all other activities are directed
462	Voice over IP; the protocol that soft phones use
463	Chief Information Officer, or CIO
464	Errors and Omissions Insurance
465	A plan that documents how an organization will prevent disruptions and continue operating at a strategical level with minimal or no downtime after a serious event happens
466	The act of making sure that an organization's security policies, standards and procedures are being followed
467	Infrastructure as a Service, or IaaS
468	The people who interact with IT systems on a daily basis and enact changes as needed
469	ISO 27004
470	- Locate all assets and build a threat profile - Locate all network paths and IT components required for each asset - Assign risk to each asset and decide what to do about it

Section 2

471	Define: Markov Analysis
472	Define: Biased Assimilation
473	What are the seven things that culture is comprised of?
474	Define: Malware
475	Define: ISO 27000 Series
476	Define: Measured Service
477	Define: Risk Evaluation Phase
478	What are the six areas program management must be evaluate?
479	Term: The ability to protect information from improper modification
480	What will be true when we have achieved effective risk management?

Section 2

175

471	A risk approach that assumes future events are not necessarily tied to past events; in this way we can examine systems that can exist in multiple states simultaneously
472	Encountered when we accept only facts that support our current position or perspective
473	- Organizational behavior - How people influence the organization's structure so that work can get done - Attitudes - Norms - How well teams work together - The existence or lack of turf wars - Geographic dispersion
474	Malicious software that a user installs without knowing its true evil purpose
475	A set of standards to help organizations create and implement a valid security plan
476	Occurs when customers are charged-per-use
477	A phase of risk assessment where we look at the impact from each risk and decide if it falls within an acceptable range based on our risk appetite, tolerance and capacity.
478	- Program objectives - Compliance requirements - Program management - Security operations management - Technical security management - Resource levels
479	Integrity
480	- We can handle complexity - Risk appetite and tolerance have been dictated by senior management - The information security manager has the authority to carry out his or her function - All Important assets have been identified, classified and have an owner - Assets have been prioritized

Section 2

176

481	Define: Long-Haul Network Diversity
482	Term: A security access control using groups to make security administration easier
483	Term: An organization who owns the CISM certification, and who has created the Risk IT Framework.
484	What three steps does the BIA follow?
485	Term: The percentage of an asset's value that is likely to be destroyed by a given risk
486	Term: The tendency to overestimate the extent to which other people share our own views or beliefs
487	Define: High-Availability
488	Term: An activity used to determine information security deficiencies in terms of controls and compliancy
489	Term: The act of measuring policies, procedures and controls to ensure they are being enacted and effective
490	Term: Software that runs on a computer and detects malicious software either attempting to install or that have already been installed
491	Term: An incident response team model in which we have only one team
492	Term: A process that looks at all business functions, and for the most important figures out what resources are critical for that function to continue operating
493	What is the standard to which many organizations choose to be assessed and certified against?
494	Define: Role
495	Define: Risk Tolerance
496	What is the BMIS dynamic relationship between Organization and People?
497	Define: Status Quo Bias

Section 2

481	A network continuity method that subscribes to two or more network service providers at the same time
482	Discretionary access control, or DAC
483	ISACA
484	• Gather assessment material • Analyze the information • Document the result and present recommendations
485	Exposure Factor, or EF
486	False Consensus
487	A storage solution in which we have two systems, but only one is in active use and the second is not necessarily kept up to date in real-time
488	Audit
489	Compliance
490	Antivirus
491	Central IRT Model
492	Business Resource Dependency Assessment
493	The ISO 27000 series
494	A title given to someone based on their job function
495	The amount of deviation from the risk appetite a business considers acceptable
496	Culture
497	A phenomenon in which a person will favor a known approach even when it has been demonstrated to be vastly ineffective

Section 2

498	Term: All activities and resources that provide information security services to an organization
499	Term: A monetary value assigned to an asset
500	What are the two states a control can default to when it detects a malfunction?
501	What are the six outcomes that will tell us if our information security governance is working?
502	Term: The last step in handling an incident, and carries out mitigation, containment, and recovery
503	Term: Insurance that protects against employee or agent theft and embezzlement
504	Term: A value that tells us how well a process is performing relative to reaching a goal
505	Define: ISO 27001
506	Define: Security Awareness Trainers
507	Define: Monte-Carlo Analysis
508	Term: An incident response team model in we simply outsource at least a portion of the security team
509	Term: Attributes on metrics used to calculate an overall value for prioritization
510	Term: Indicates the time between an event and impact
511	Term: The amount of risk a business can absorb without ceasing to exist
512	Define: Antispam Device
513	Term: The beliefs and resulting behaviors that are expected and are viewed as normal within the company
514	Term: A risk approach in which numbers are assigned to both impact and likelihood

498	Information Security Program
499	Asset Value, or AV
500	Fail unsecure and fail secure
501	<ul><li>Strategically aligned</li><li>Managing risk</li><li>Delivered value</li><li>Optimized resources</li><li>Measuring performance</li><li>Integration</li></ul>
502	Incident Response
503	Fidelity Insurance
504	Key Performance Indicator, or KPI
505	Part of the ISO 27000 series that lays out requirements for an information security management system, or ISMS
506	The people who understand risk management goals and processes and create training materials and programs to spread this knowledge to the appropriate employees
507	A risk approach that combines known risk with sources of uncertainty and calculates possible outcomes
508	Outsourced IRT Model
509	Metametrics
510	Proximity
511	Risk Capacity
512	A server component designed to detect and delete email SPAM
513	Culture
514	Quantitative Analysis

Section 2

515	What is the last line of defense for cost-effective risk management?
516	Define: Deterrent Control
517	Define: Detective Control
518	Define: Authentication
519	Define: Procedural Control
520	Define: Architecture Development Method, or ADM
521	What does the SMART acronym stand for?
522	Define: Annualized Rate of Occurrence, or ARO
523	Define: Right-To-Inspect
524	Define: Quantitative Analysis
525	Define: Incident Response Plan, or IRP
526	Define: Technical Threat
527	Define: Warm Site
528	Define: Policy
529	Define: Information Security Resource Management
530	What are the four elements of FAIR?
531	Term: A recovery site that is an always active duplicate site
532	Define: Factor Analysis of Information Risk, or FAIR

515	Incident management
516	A control capable of providing warnings that can deter a potential compromise
517	A control that warns us of attempted or successful violations of a security policy
518	The action of proving who we claim we are
519	A control that oversees or reports on a process and includes the procedures and operations of that process
520	A portion of TOGAF that is used to drive progress, and contains 9 phases and a central block
521	<ul><li>Specific</li><li>Measurable</li><li>Attainable</li><li>Relevant</li><li>Timely</li></ul>
522	The number of times a threat on a single asset is expected to happen in a single year
523	A contract clause requiring little or no advanced notice of an inspection
524	A risk approach in which numbers are assigned to both impact and likelihood
525	The operational component of incident management
526	A type of threat that includes fire, electrical failure, gas or water leakage
527	A recovery site that has the complete infrastructure ready to go, but usually is not able to operate at the capacity of the original site
528	A high-level statement of what senior management expects and will dictate the direction in which we are heading
529	The processes to plan, allocate and control resources
530	<ul><li>Taxonomy</li><li>Method for measuring</li><li>Computational engine</li><li>Simulation model</li></ul>
531	Mirror Site
532	An approach that allows us to decompose risk and understand the underlying components

533	Term: A set of standards to help organizations create and implement a valid security plan
534	Term: An unambiguous list of steps required to accomplish a task
535	Define: Corporate Governance
536	Term: A risk approach that is a top-down model where we start with an event and look for possible causes for that event to occur
537	Define: Managerial Control
538	Define: Vulnerability Management
539	Define: ISO 27002
540	Term: The likelihood that a threat agent will exploit a vulnerability combined with the damage that could result
541	What is the BMIS dynamic relationship between Process and People?
542	Define: The Federal Information Security Modernization Act, or FISMA
543	Term: A recovery site configured exactly like the primary site and can be anything from a hot site to a reciprocal agreement with another company
544	Term: A control that oversees or reports on a process and includes the procedures and operations of that process
545	Define: Security Team
546	Term: A methodology to look at complex life cycles from concept to retirement
547	Term: The loss we will encounter if we experienced a single instance of a specific risk
548	Term: Mounting evidence that something nefarious is going on in the organization's network and systems
549	Term: A control that remediates or reverses an impact after it has been felt
550	Term: A type of threat that results from man-made actions
551	Define: Metric
552	Define: Procedure

Section 2

533	ISO 27000 Series
534	Procedure
535	A process that sets the strategic direction of a business by defining goals
536	Fault Tree Analysis
537	Another name for a procedural control
538	Part of the incident management capability represented by proactive identification, monitoring and repair of any weakness
539	Part of the ISO 27000 series that provides best practices for information security controls
540	Risk
541	Emergence
542	A federal law passed in 2002 that provides a framework to protect federal agencies from security breaches
543	Duplicate Site
544	Procedural Control
545	An incident response team that takes care of all security concerns, including monitoring the security of systems and communications
546	Probabilistic Risk Assessment, or PRA
547	Single Loss Expectancy, or SLE
548	Emerging Threat
549	Corrective Control
550	Man-Made Threat
551	Created by comparing two data points to each other
552	An unambiguous list of steps required to accomplish a task

Section 2

553	Define: Probabilistic Risk Assessment, or PRA
554	Define: Value Delivery
555	Define: Security as a Service, or SecaaS
556	What is the most important aspect to consider with how the information security and IT departments report up through the organization?
557	Define: Business and Functional Managers
558	What are the three control technological categories?
559	Term: The person who is responsible for security programs creating a methodology to identify and manage risk, usually including IT systems
560	Define: Delphi Method
561	Term: A network continuity method that routes traffic through split or duplicate cables
562	Term: A control that makes up for a weakness in another control
563	Define: The Center for Internet Security, or CIS
564	Define: Emergency Action Team
565	Define: Physical Control
566	Term: An architectural category which are very flexible and open
567	Define: Anchoring
568	Term: A risk approach in which the magnitude of the impact and likelihood of the potential consequences are arranged on a 2-dimensional matrix
569	What four things related to risk does a BIA do?

Section 2

553	A methodology to look at complex life cycles from concept to retirement
554	Occurs when the investment in security provides the greatest support for business goals
555	A cloud-based offering providing a way to outsource security processes
556	Each department must report up through a different executive to avoid conflict of interests.
557	The managers responsible for business operations and the IT procurement processes
558	<ul><li>Native</li><li>Supplemental</li><li>Support</li></ul>
559	Information Security Manager
560	A risk approach that arrives at a consensus by asking a question to a group, tallying and revealing the anonymous results to the entire group, and then repeating until there is agreement.
561	Diverse Routing
562	Compensating Control
563	An organization that released a document in 2010 called The CIS Security Metrics based on the consensus of 150 industry professionals
564	An incident response team that deals with fires and other emergency scenarios
565	A control that can physically restrict access to a facility or hardware
566	Frameworks
567	The tendency to tie future estimates to a past estimate, even if there is no link between the two numbers.
568	Qualitative Analysis
569	<ul><li>It determines the impact of losing the availability of any resource</li><li>It establishes the escalation of that loss over time</li><li>It identifies the resources needed to recover</li><li>It prioritizes the recovery of processes and supporting systems</li></ul>

Section 2

570	What are the five essential characteristics of cloud computing?
571	Term: A set of detailed practices for managing IT services with a special focus on aligning those services with the needs of business
572	Why does Enterprise Resource Planning, or ERP, systems deserve special attention?
573	Term: A risk approach that combines known risk with sources of uncertainty and calculates possible outcomes
574	Define: Paper Tests
575	Define: Cascading Risk
576	Define: Administrative Control
577	Define: Hybrid Model
578	Define: The Business Model for Information Security, or BMIS
579	Term: A method to address a need separate from the bulk of the organization
580	Term: The minimum security level across the entire organization
581	Term: A cloud-based offering taking on the responsibility of hosting and maintaining a disaster recovery solution
582	Term: A cloud-based offering for identity management
583	Term: A plan test category which is the same as a full interruption test
584	Term: A network continuity method that subscribes to two or more network service providers at the same time
585	Define: Data Storage and Data Analytics as a Service
586	Term: Encountered when we experience pressure for agreement in team-based cultures.
587	Can we transfer legal impact of a risk?
588	Define: General Control

570	• On-demand self-service • Accessible over a broadband network • Computer resources are pooled • Elasticity • Measured service
571	Information Technology Infrastructure Library, or ITIL
572	Because the compromise of this single system can disrupt operations across the entire organization
573	Monte-Carlo Analysis
574	A plan test category which covers checklist reviews and structured walkthroughs
575	Occurs when a single failure leads to a chain reaction of other failures
576	Another name for a procedural control
577	Occurs when a private cloud connects across the public Internet into another application
578	A business-oriented approach to information security that models complex relationships using system theory
579	Sub-Policy
580	Baseline Security
581	Disaster Recovery as a Service, or DRaaS
582	Identity as a Service, or IDaaS
583	Full Operational Test
584	Long-Haul Network Diversity
585	A cloud-based offering that delivers storage and analysis of huge amounts of data
586	Groupthink
587	No
588	Any control that is not a countermeasure.

Section 2

589	Define: The Open Group Architecture Framework, or TOGAF
590	Define: Design
591	Define: Risk Management Strategy
592	Define: Predisposing Conditions
593	What are the three ways in which we can group controls?
594	Define: Mirror Site
595	Term: Another name for a stage gate
596	Term: Metrics that are comprised of technical and procedural metrics such as existing vulnerabilities and the progress of our patch management processes
597	Define: Single Loss Expectancy, or SLE
598	Define: Community Cloud
599	Term: The application of multiple control layers such that if a layer fails, it does not cause the failure of the next layer as well
600	Term: An insurance policy an organization purchases to cover itself in the event that RTO is exceeded.
601	Term: The location and delivery of information in response to a request in which the company is legally bound to comply with
602	Term: Unwanted software that is annoying but normally harmless
603	Define: Selective Recall
604	What are the four Balanced Scorecard perspectives?

Section 2

189

589	A framework for enterprise architecture that covers four areas, called architecture domains
590	How an organization implements strategy and includes processes, culture and architecture
591	The plan to achieve risk management goals
592	Scenarios which may lead to the rapid or unpredictable emergence of new vulnerabilities
593	<ul><li>Methods</li><li>Categories</li><li>Technological categories</li></ul>
594	A recovery site that is an always active duplicate site
595	Kill Point
596	Operational Metrics
597	The loss we will encounter if we experienced a single instance of a specific risk
598	A private cloud that a select few other companies can access
599	Defense-In-Depth
600	Business Interruption Insurance
601	E-discovery
602	Adware
603	Occurs when we remember only facts and experiences that support our current assumptions
604	<ul><li>Learning and growth</li><li>Business process</li><li>Customer</li><li>Financial</li></ul>

Section 2

605	What are the three categories of plan tests?
606	What are the three steps to follow when selecting controls?
607	Define: Compensating Control
608	What is the advantage of using a quantitative approach to assessing impact?
609	Term: A type of threat such as natural disasters
610	Term: A cloud-based offering that comes into play when a hybrid cloud model is used
611	Term: An organization that released a document in 2010 called The CIS Security Metrics based on the consensus of 150 industry professionals
612	What are the four architecture domains in TOGAF?
613	What are the five components of a good security review process?
614	Define: Parallel Test
615	What does RACI stand for?
616	Define: Redundant Array of Inexpensive Disks, or RAID
617	Term: The potential loss when a vulnerability is exploited by a threat

Section 2

191

605	- Paper - Preparedness - Full Operational
606	- Determine acceptable risk and risk tolerance - Determine control objectives based on acceptable risk levels - Determine requirements for controls based on the objectives
607	A control that makes up for a weakness in another control
608	It supports a cost/benefit analysis
609	Environmental Threat
610	Integration Platform as a Service, or IPaaS
611	The Center for Internet Security, or CIS
612	- Business architecture - Applications architecture - Data architecture - Technical architecture
613	- An objective - A scope - A list of constraints - An approach - A result
614	A plan test in which the recovery site is brought up to a state of operational readiness, but operations at the primary site continue
615	- Responsible - Accountable - Consulted - Informed
616	A disk configuration providing great redundancy and performance improvements by writing data to multiple disks simultaneously
617	Exposure

Section 2

618	What is the relationship between risk appetite, tolerance and capacity?
619	Define: GRC
620	What are the two most prevalent challenges facing a security manager?
621	Define: Business Impact Analysis, or BIA
622	What term represents the 'laws' of an organization?
623	Define: Red-Amber-Green Report
624	Term: A plan test category which covers checklist reviews and structured walkthroughs
625	Define: Cloud Access Security Brokers, or CASBs
626	Define: Systemic Risk
627	Define: Confidentiality
628	What are four challenges when dealing with third-party entities?
629	Define: Advanced Persistent Threat (APT)
630	Define: Infrastructure as a Service, or IaaS
631	Term: A control that warns us of attempted or successful violations of a security policy
632	Term: The foundation upon which information systems are deployed
633	Term: Voice over IP; the protocol that soft phones use
634	Term: A storage solution in which we have two systems, but only one is in active use and the second is not necessarily kept up to date in real-time
635	Term: Where we want to be
636	Term: An attribute attached to the target

618	risk appetite + risk tolerance <= risk capacity
619	The trifecta of governance, risk management and compliance
620	- A view that security can be fixed with technology - Increased security simply makes my job harder
621	An analysis that helps us to understand what assets are important, and what their loss will mean to us
622	Standards
623	A report that uses color to quickly convey status
624	Paper Tests
625	Tools that provide an easy and comprehensive way to secure the path between a company and hosted cloud services
626	Represents a negative event affecting a large part of the area or industry
627	Prevents unauthorized disclosure of information
628	- Cultural differences - Technology incompatibilities - How incidences are responded to - The level of acceptable BC and DR
629	A skilled external attacker who is willing to invest considerable time and resources into bypassing an organization's network and system security controls.
630	A cloud-based offering that provides the customer with a ready-made network, storage and servers
631	Detective Control
632	Infrastructure
633	VoIP
634	High-Availability
635	Desired State
636	Visibility

Section 2

637	What are the minimum four things a BIA must do?
638	What are the six COBIT 5 PAM levels?
639	Term: The likelihood that a threat will exploit a vulnerability
640	Define: Strategically Alignment
641	Define: Incident Handling
642	Define: Transparency
643	Define: Disaster Recovery Plan, or DRP
644	Term: A security access control that looks at the classification of the requested resource and compares it to the security clearance of the user
645	Define: Environmental Threat
646	Term: Allows separate networks to talk to each other by 'routing' the traffic between them
647	Term: A control technology category representing technology that is added to an information system after the fact
648	Define: Allowable Interruption Window, or AIW
649	Define: System Theory
650	Define: Maximum Tolerable Outage, or MTO
651	Define: Recovery Point Objective, or RPO

637	<ul><li>Determine the loss resulting from some function no longer being available</li><li>Figure out how that loss will escalate over time</li><li>Identify the minimum resources needed to recover from that loss</li><li>Prioritize the recovery of processes and systems for all losses</li></ul>
638	<ul><li>Level 0 - Incomplete Process</li><li>Level 1 - Performed Process</li><li>Level 2 - Managed Process</li><li>Level 3 - Established Process</li><li>Level 4 - Predictable Process</li><li>Level 5 - Optimizing Process</li></ul>
639	Probability
640	Occurs when information security lines up with our business strategy
641	A service that covers all processes or tasks associated with handling events and incidents
642	Achieved when all stakeholders can easily understand how a security mechanism is supposed to work
643	A plan that documents how we will quickly restore data, applications and core services that run our business after a serious event happens
644	Mandatory access control, or MAC
645	A type of threat such as natural disasters
646	Router
647	Supplemental Control
648	The amount of time normal operations can be down before the organization faces major financial problems that threaten its existence
649	An approach that views a system as a complete functioning unit - not simply the sum of its parts
650	The maximum time that an organization can operate in an alternate or recovery mode until normal operations are resumed
651	The amount of data we can stand to permanently lose in case of interruption in terms of time, usually hours or days.

Section 2

652	Term: How an organization implements strategy and includes processes, culture and architecture
653	Define: Exception Process
654	Term: Occurs when computing capabilities are provisioned without any type of human interaction
655	Term: A plan test category which covers simulation and parallel tests
656	Define: Integration Platform as a Service, or IPaaS
657	Term: A control having documentation reflecting its procedures and how well it has been maintained
658	Define: Exploit
659	Define: Relocation Team
660	Define: Inherent Risk
661	What are the three metric categories?
662	What are the three types of threats we most often encounter?
663	Term: A subset of enterprise architecture designed to give a jump-start on designing an information security program
664	Define: Fidelity Coverage Policies
665	Term: A network continuity method that protects the communications infrastructure connected directly to a facility
666	Define: Voice Recovery
667	Term: An approach that groups resources into separate 'compartments', with each requiring a unique authorization control
668	Define: Formal Control
669	What is the BMIS dynamic relationship between Organization and Process?
670	Define: Risk Acceptance

652	Design
653	Created when we encounter a standard for which we cannot create a process
654	On-Demand Self-Service
655	Preparedness Test
656	A cloud-based offering that comes into play when a hybrid cloud model is used
657	Formal Control
658	Occurs when a vulnerability is taken advantage of by an attacker
659	An incident response team that moves operations from the affected site to an alternate site, and then back once the original site has been restored
660	A risk prior to mitigation.
661	• Strategic • Tactical • Operational
662	• Environmental • Technical • Man-made
663	Enterprise Information Security Architecture, or EISA
664	Insurance that covers loss from dishonest or fraudulent acts by employees
665	Last-Mile Circuit Protection
666	A network continuity method that provides redundancy for voice lines
667	Compartmentalize to Minimize Damage
668	A control having documentation reflecting its procedures and how well it has been maintained
669	Governance
670	Occurs when an organization decides that no action is required for a specific risk

Section 2

671	Term: A process that sets the strategic direction of a business by defining goals
672	What are the five CMMI Levels?
673	Define: Enforcement Procedure
674	Term: An agreement between one or more businesses that promise to share their data centers and systems in the event one of the partners experiences an outage
675	Term: The plan test phase which sets the stage for the actual test
676	Define: Tactical Metrics
677	Term: A type of threat that includes fire, electrical failure, gas or water leakage
678	Define: Preparedness Test
679	Define: Test Phase
680	When dealing with risk taxonomy, what are four characteristics we need to look at?
681	Term: A measure of how accessible an IT system or process is to its end users
682	Term: An approach that segments all resources so that we can increase access as-needed
683	Define: Identity
684	Term: A portion of TOGAF that is used to drive progress, and contains 9 phases and a central block
685	Define: Risk Appetite
686	What are the three types of measurements we can use for policies, standards and guidelines?

671	Corporate Governance
672	- Level 1 - Initial - Level 2 - Managed - Level 3 - Defied - Level 4 - Quantitatively Managed - Level 5 - Optimizing
673	A procedure that makes sure another procedure is being followed
674	Reciprocal Agreement
675	Pretest Phase
676	Another name for management metrics
677	Technical Threat
678	A plan test category which covers simulation and parallel tests
679	The plan test phase where the emergency is simulated, and people, systems and processes are moved to the recovery site to the extent the test allows
680	- The frequency with which threat agents contact assets at-risk - The probability of action by threat agents - The probability of success by threat agents - The type and severity of the impact to assets
681	Availability
682	Principle of Least Privilege
683	Something that uniquely identifies the user, such as a user name, email address or thumbprint
684	Architecture Development Method, or ADM
685	The amount of risk a business is willing to incur
686	- Metrics - Boundaries - Processes

Section 2

687	Define: Groupthink
688	What are five methods we can use to analyze risk?
689	Term: A disk configuration providing great redundancy and performance improvements by writing data to multiple disks simultaneously
690	Term: The person who performs the same functions as the security manager, but holds greater authority and reports to the CEO, COO or the board of directors
691	What are the four types of metrics we need to collect during testing?
692	Define: Incident Management
693	Term: Represents the true cost to own an asset, as opposed to just the cost to initially acquire it
694	Term: The architecture that is to be built
695	Term: A network hosted entirely inside of a company's intranet and is not accessible externally.
696	Term: A control that always contains some type of technology whether it is hardware or software
697	Term: Another name for a procedural control
698	Define: Defense-In-Depth
699	Term: A plan test in which team members implement the plan on paper
700	Term: A plan test in which all steps are reviewed
701	Term: Part of the ISO 27000 series that lays out requirements for an information security management system, or ISMS

Section 2

201

687	Encountered when we experience pressure for agreement in team-based cultures.
688	• Qualitative Analysis • Semiquantitative Analysis • Quantitative Analysis • Value at Risk • Operationally Critical Threat Asset and Vulnerability Evaluation (OCTAVE)
689	Redundant Array of Inexpensive Disks, or RAID
690	Chief Information Security Officer, or CISO
691	• Elapsed time for completion of each major component • The amount of work performed at the backup site • Percentages that reflect the number of vital records, supplies and equipment successfully delivered to the backup site • The accuracy of data entry and processing cycles at the recovery site
692	Ensures that incidents are detected, recorded and managed to limit impacts
693	Total Cost of Ownership
694	Reference Architecture
695	Private Cloud
696	Technical Control
697	Managerial Control
698	The application of multiple control layers such that if a layer fails, it does not cause the failure of the next layer as well
699	Structured Walkthrough Test
700	Checklist Review Test
701	ISO 27001

Section 2

202

702	Define: Antivirus	
703	Define: Measured Point	
704	Define: Central IRT Model	
705	Term: An incident response team that moves operations from the affected site to an alternate site, and then back once the original site has been restored	
706	Term: A tool that gathers logs from across the network and combines the data into a single database	
707	Term: A risk approach that is a bottom-up model that attempts to predict the future by reasoning through various events and calculating the probability of possible outcomes	
708	What is the goal of Incident management?	
709	Term: Insurance that reimburses lost profit because of an IT malfunction or security incident causing the loss of computing resources	
710	Define: Standard	
711	Term: Scenarios which may lead to the rapid or unpredictable emergence of new vulnerabilities	
712	Define: Baseline Security	
713	Define: Enterprise Governance	
714	Term: Similar to Biased Assimilation, but we go one step further and attack anyone presenting facts that conflict with our own	
715	Term: A federal law passed in 2002 that provides a framework to protect federal agencies from security breaches	
716	Term: The maximum time that an organization can operate in an alternate or recovery mode until normal operations are resumed	
717	Define: Mobile Site	
718	Term: An architectural category which are actually small-scale representations of the actual implementation	

Section 2

702	Software that runs on a computer and detects malicious software either attempting to install or that have already been installed
703	A measurement taken after a reference point later and is used to see how far off we are, or how far we have come
704	An incident response team model in which we have only one team
705	Relocation Team
706	Security Information and Event Manager, or SIEM
707	Event Tree Analysis
708	To prevent incidents from becoming problems, and problems from becoming disasters.
709	Business Interruption Insurance
710	Tells us how to carry out a policy
711	Predisposing Conditions
712	The minimum security level across the entire organization
713	A process that watches over the entire organization or business
714	Biased Evaluation
715	The Federal Information Security Modernization Act, or FISMA
716	Maximum Tolerable Outage, or MTO
717	A recovery site that is a specially designed trailer that can be quickly moved to a business location when needed
718	Reference Models

Section 2

719	Define: Steering Committee
720	What are the four groups that need tailored communications?
721	Term: Insurance that covers loss from dishonest or fraudulent acts by employees
722	Define: Governance
723	What can tend to weaken a procedure?
724	Define: Event Tree Analysis
725	Term: A framework for enterprise architecture that covers four areas, called architecture domains
726	Term: A US federal law passed in 2002 that puts requirements on all publicly traded businesses to encourage transparency
727	Define: System and Information Owners
728	Define: Corrective Control
729	Define: Strategy
730	Term: The action of addressing known risks until they are at acceptable levels, identifying potential risks and associated impacts, and prioritizing both against our business goals
731	Term: An incident response team that deals with fires and other emergency scenarios
732	Term: Encountered when we accept only facts that support our current position or perspective
733	Define: Threat agent
734	Term: A report that uses color to quickly convey status
735	Term: A service that covers all processes or tasks associated with handling events and incidents

719	A collective made up of senior representatives from all impacted groups
720	• Senior management • Business process owners • Other management personnel • Remaining employees
721	Fidelity Coverage Policies
722	The act of creating a plan on how a company will achieve a goal and then making sure everyone executes that plan
723	Too many uses of discretionary tasks
724	A risk approach that is a bottom-up model that attempts to predict the future by reasoning through various events and calculating the probability of possible outcomes
725	The Open Group Architecture Framework, or TOGAF
726	The Sarbanes-Oxley Act (SOX)
727	The people who ensure controls are in place to address CIA, and who must approve changes to IT systems
728	A control that remediates or reverses an impact after it has been felt
729	A plan of action to achieve a goal
730	Risk Management
731	Emergency Action Team
732	Biased Assimilation
733	A person or process that exploits a vulnerability
734	Red-Amber-Green Report
735	Incident Handling

Section 2

736	When using load balancing or clustering, what must we be careful to do?
737	Define: Data Architecture Domain
738	Term: Malicious software that a user installs without knowing its true evil purpose
739	What is the advantage of using a qualitative approach to assessing impact?
740	What are the four types of cloud deployment models?
741	Which security access control is used in high-security implementations such as a military system?
742	Define: Bayesian Analysis
743	Define: Guideline
744	Term: Insurance that covers loss or damage to media during transport
745	Term: A recovery site that is fully configured and can be ready to operate in a number of hours
746	Define: Information
747	Define: Assurance
748	Define: The Sarbanes-Oxley Act (SOX)
749	Define: Need-to-Know
750	What three items must the security manager take care of prior to a test?
751	Term: An architectural category which dictates the processes used for each element
752	What is the minimal training that incident response teams should go through?

736	Ensure that all load can be handled by either system by itself
737	The TOGAF architecture domain which describes the structure of logical and physical data, and management resources
738	Malware
739	It prioritizes risk and identifies areas for immediate improvement
740	• Private cloud • Community cloud • Public cloud • Hybrid model
741	MAC
742	A risk approach that looks at historical data and calculates the probability of risk
743	Contains information that is helpful when executing procedures
744	Media Transportation Insurance
745	Hot Site
746	Data having meaning and purpose
747	Being able to manage security risks by keeping vulnerabilities and threats to a level that we can live with
748	A US federal law passed in 2002 that puts requirements on all publicly traded businesses to encourage transparency
749	A security approach that requires a person to not only have the proper authority to access resources, but also a valid need to do so
750	• The risk of disruption is minimized • The business accepts the risk of testing • The organization can restore operation at any point during testing
751	Process Models
752	• Induction • Mentoring on roles, responsibilities and procedures • On-the-job training • Formal training

Section 2

753	Term: A control that can physically restrict access to a facility or hardware
754	Define: Coordinating IRT Model
755	Term: An organization providing a framework called the 'COSO Framework'.
756	What are some of the best controls?
757	What might happen if we mitigate a risk?
758	Term: Shown when we act to ensure things don't go wrong
759	Define: Direct Attached Storage, or DAS
760	Term: A department that oversees all projects
761	Term: A cloud-based offering that manages operating systems, middleware and other run-time components
762	Term: A value that tells us after the fact if an IT process has achieved its goal
763	Term: Occurs when resource can rapidly scale up or down in response to real-time business needs
764	What are six elements of the initial business case?
765	Term: A tool used to capture both the current and future desired state for information security
766	What storage solutions can RAID be used with?

753	Physical Control
754	An incident response team model in in which we have multiple distributed teams that manage and implement responses but rely upon a single central team providing all guidance and policy decisions
755	The Committee of Sponsoring Organizations of the Treadway Commission, or COSO
756	- Strong access controls - Limiting access to need-to-know - Network segmentation - Effective termination procedures - Good monitoring
757	Another risk will increase, or perhaps even be created
758	Due Care
759	A data storage device that is connected directly to a server or client
760	Project Management Office, or PMO
761	Platform as a Service, or PaaS
762	Key Goal Indicator, or KGI
763	Elasticity
764	- Project scope - Current analysis - Requirements - Approach - Evaluation - Review
765	COBIT 5 Process Assessment Model (PAM)
766	DAS, NAS or SAN solutions

Section 2

767	Term: Insurance which reimburses to the business for expenses incurred in maintaining operations at a facility that experiences damage.
768	What are the three phases of risk assessment?
769	If a procedural task is discretionary, what terms should we use?
770	Term: A plan test in which team members role-play a simulated disaster without activating the recovery site
771	What are the four incident response team models?
772	Term: Information that has been absorbed
773	What four things must a procedure define?
774	Define: Software as a Service, or SaaS
775	Term: Measures the proficiency of the attacker and informs us of potential targets
776	Term: A measure of the impact if we accidentally disclose information
777	Term: A strategy to prevent, recover and continue from disasters
778	Term: A risk approach that arrives at a consensus by asking a question to a group, tallying and revealing the anonymous results to the entire group, and then repeating until there is agreement.
779	Term: A plan that documents how we will quickly restore data, applications and core services that run our business after a serious event happens
780	What is the BMIS dynamic relationship People and Technology?
781	Term: A form of malware but specifically watches whatever the user does, usually to steal credentials
782	What are the three primary goals for a BIA?

Section 2

767	Extra Expense Policy
768	- Identification - Analysis - Evaluation
769	'May' and 'can'
770	Simulation Test
771	- Central IRT model - Distributed IRT model - Coordinating IRT model - Outsourced IRT model
772	Knowledge
773	- Required conditions before execution - Information displayed - The expected outcome - What to do when the unexpected happens
774	A cloud-based offering that is an application that someone hosts and maintains.
775	Skill
776	Sensitivity
777	Business Continuity
778	Delphi Method
779	Disaster Recovery Plan, or DRP
780	Human Factors
781	Spyware
782	- Prioritize the criticality of business process - Estimate the amount of downtime - Identify resource requirements

Section 2

783	What are the main two factors leading to improperly configured systems?
784	Term: The amount of risk a business is willing to incur
785	What are the 10 components in TOGAF ADM?
786	Term: Occurs when the investment in security provides the greatest support for business goals
787	Define: Desired State
788	Term: Achieved when all stakeholders can easily understand how a security mechanism is supposed to work
789	Term: Compliance where we are obligated by a contract to remain in compliance
790	Term: Occurs when multiple failures happen within a very short time frame of each other
791	Term: A contract clause allowing the customer to initiate an audit given sufficient notice to the vendor
792	Term: A security approach that requires a person to not only have the proper authority to access resources, but also a valid need to do so
793	What are the two primary purposes for a contract?
794	Define: Intrusion Prevention System, or IPS
795	Define: Culture
796	Define: Chief Information Security Officer, or CISO

Section 2

784	Risk Appetite
785	- Preliminary - Architecture vision - Business architecture - Information systems - Technology architecture - Opportunities and solutions - Migration planning - Implementation governance - Architecture change management - Central requirements management block
786	Value Delivery
787	Where we want to be
788	Transparency
789	Contractual Compliance
790	Contagious Risk
791	Right-To-Audit
792	Need-to-Know
793	- To clearly spell out rights and responsibilities - To provide a way to handle disagreements after the contract is signed
794	An IDS that will actively try and stop an attack that is underway
795	The beliefs and resulting behaviors that are expected and are viewed as normal within the company
796	The person who performs the same functions as the security manager, but holds greater authority and reports to the CEO, COO or the board of directors

Section 2

797	Term: A single real-world instance of a vulnerability being exploited by a threat agent
798	Term: The recovery of all critical business processes required to resume operations
799	What are the five steps when testing a plan?
800	Term: A location where we move operations after the original site has been compromised
801	Define: Availability
802	Define: Alternative Routing
803	Term: Measures the type of motivation the attacker has
804	Term: Part of the incident management capability represented by proactive identification, monitoring and repair of any weakness
805	What is one of the downsides to a BIA?
806	Define: Disaster Recovery
807	Term: Contains information that is helpful when executing procedures
808	Term: An incident response team that assesses the physical damage and decides what is a total loss or can be salvaged
809	If there is risk associated with taking some kind of action, is there also risk associated with not taking that action?
810	Term: Occurs when customers are charged-per-use
811	Define: The Control Objectives for Information and Related Technologies, or COBIT
812	Define: E-discovery

Section 2

215

797	Exposure
798	Business Recovery
799	• Develop test objectives • Execute the test • Evaluate the test • Create recommendations to improve effectiveness • Ensure recommendations are implemented
800	Recovery Site
801	A measure of how accessible an IT system or process is to its end users
802	A network continuity method that routes information through an alternate medium such as copper cable or fiber optics
803	Motivation
804	Vulnerability Management
805	All assessments tend to be 'worse-case' and end up being inflated
806	The recovery of IT systems after a disruption
807	Guideline
808	Damage Assessment Team
809	Yes.
810	Measured Service
811	A framework created by ISACA and is geared specifically to IT
812	The location and delivery of information in response to a request in which the company is legally bound to comply with

Section 2

813	Beyond SMART, what other attributes comprise a good litmus test for metrics?
814	Define: Business Interruption Insurance
815	What is the BMIS dynamic relationship between Organization and Technology?
816	Term: Tells us how to carry out a policy
817	Define: Trust No One
818	What five actions take place during risk analysis?
819	Define: Integrity
820	Term: An incident response team model in in which we have multiple distributed teams that manage and implement responses but rely upon a single central team providing all guidance and policy decisions
821	Define: Due Care
822	Define: NIST SP 800-55
823	Term: Represents a negative event affecting a large part of the area or industry
824	Define: Infrastructure
825	Define: Total Cost of Ownership
826	Term: A risk approach that assumes future events are not necessarily tied to past events; in this way we can examine systems that can exist in multiple states simultaneously
827	Term: Insurance that covers losses incurred as a result of a cyberattack
828	What do you get when you combine overconfidence with optimism?

813	<ul><li>Accurate</li><li>Cost-Effective</li><li>Repeatable</li><li>Predictive</li><li>Actionable</li></ul>
814	Insurance that reimburses lost profit because of an IT malfunction or security incident causing the loss of computing resources
815	Architecture
816	Standard
817	A design strategy that does not trust any one person to follow the proper procedures when administrating a system
818	<ul><li>Examine all risk sources</li><li>Determine exposure</li><li>Determine consequences</li><li>Determine likelihood</li><li>Identify all existing controls</li></ul>
819	The ability to protect information from improper modification
820	Coordinating IRT Model
821	Shown when we act to ensure things don't go wrong
822	A standard that aligns with the security controls listed in NIST SP 800-53
823	Systemic Risk
824	The foundation upon which information systems are deployed
825	Represents the true cost to own an asset, as opposed to just the cost to initially acquire it
826	Markov Analysis
827	Cybersecurity Insurance
828	Estimates that are unrealistically precise and overly optimistic

Section 2

829	Term: The foundation on top of which the entire company is built
830	Term: Insurance that covers the actual cash value of papers and records that have been disclosed, or physically damaged or lost
831	Term: A measure of how stable the conditions giving rise to risk are.
832	Define: Valuable Papers and Records Policies
833	Term: A cloud-based offering providing a way to outsource security processes
834	Define: Organization
835	Term: Occurs when a single failure leads to a chain reaction of other failures
836	Term: An organization authoring the ISO 2000 series, of which ISO 27001 and ISO 27002 are ones the most frequently used
837	Term: An incident response team model that supports multiple teams, each responsible for a different logical or physical segment of the infrastructure
838	Define: Annual Loss Expectancy, or ALE
839	Term: Created when we encounter a standard for which we cannot create a process
840	Term: A risk approach that creates a visual diagram with the cause of an event in the middle, representing the 'knot' of a bow tie, with triggers, controls and consequences branching off of the 'knot'.
841	Term: The act of controlling who has access to sensitive information based on their identity
842	Define: Exposure Factor, or EF
843	Define: Damage Assessment Team
844	Define: Native Control
845	Term: A management system that helps organizations to create clear goals and translate them into action
846	Term: The act of striking the right balance between taking advantage of opportunities for gain while minimizing the chances of loss
847	Define: Firewall

Section 2

219

829	Enterprise Architecture Represents
830	Valuable Papers and Records Policies
831	Volatility
832	Insurance that covers the actual cash value of papers and records that have been disclosed, or physically damaged or lost
833	Security as a Service, or SecaaS
834	A network of people, assets and processes interacting with each other in defined roles and working toward a common goal
835	Cascading Risk
836	The International Organization for Standardization, or ISO
837	Distributed IRT Model
838	The amount of money we can expect to lose each year for a given risk
839	Exception Process
840	Bow Tie Analysis
841	Access Control
842	The percentage of an asset's value that is likely to be destroyed by a given risk
843	An incident response team that assesses the physical damage and decides what is a total loss or can be salvaged
844	A control technology category representing out-of-the-box capabilities
845	Balanced Scorecard
846	Risk Management
847	A network device that limits traffic to certain IP addresses and ports

Printed in Great Britain
by Amazon